Discovering Literature Series

CHALLENGING LEVEL

D0746586

Redwall

A Teaching Guide

by Mary Elizabeth Podhaizer

Illustrations by Kathy Kifer

Journey Strand

Dedicated to
Nan and Zippy

Redwall
Published by:
Avon Books
A division of
The Hearst Corporation
1350 Avenue of the Americas
New York, NY 10019

Ace Books
A division of
The Berkley Publishing Group
A member of Penguin Putnam Inc.
200 Madison Avenue
New York, NY 10016

Teaching Guide Published by:
Garlic Press
605 Powers St.
Eugene, OR 97402

ISBN 0-931993-91-1
Order Number GP-091

www.garlicpress.com

Table of Contents

Table of Contents, Cont.

NOTES TO THE TEACHER

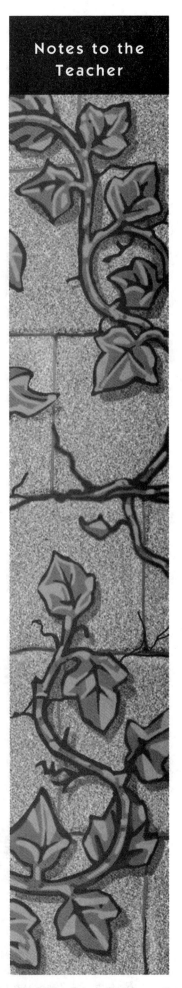

The Discovering Literature Series is designed to develop a student's appreciation for good literature and to improve reading comprehension. At the Challenging Level, we focus on a variety of reading strategies that can help students construct meaning from their experience with literature as well as make connections between their reading and the rest of their lives. The strategies reflect the demands of each literature selection. In this study guide, we will focus on beginning a book, maps and illustrations, animal fantasy/proper names, setting, plot, point of view, foreshadowing and flashback, characterization, imaging, theme, and rereading.

ORGANIZATION OF THIS LITERATURE GUIDE

Vocabulary

Each section of the guide begins with **Vocabulary** for the upcoming group of chapters. The **Chapter Vocabulary** can be either displayed on the board or on an overhead projector before each chapter is read.

Introducing the Chapter Vocabulary prior to students' reading insures that their reading is not disrupted by the frequent need to look up a word. Guide students in using one of the vocabulary exercises suggested below.

The **Chapter Vocabulary** includes definitions of key words from each chapter. To save time, students need only to copy, not look up, definitions. The more meaningful vocabulary exercises are, the more easily students will retain vocabulary. Suggestions for teaching vocabulary:

1. Finding relationships between and among words helps students learn the words better than treating them separately. Have students create a web or other graphic that shows the relationships between and among the vocabulary words. Encourage them to add other related words to their web.
2. A group of words that primarily includes nouns can be used to label a picture. For example, for Book One, Chapter 13, you might provide a landscape picture and have students label a longbow, a quarter staff, and a cudgel.
3. Have students use the words in a piece of writing, for example a poem, a one-act play, or a diary entry written from the point of view of one of the characters.
4. Have students research the etymology of the vocabulary words and keep notes on their findings.
5. Have students make and exchange crossword puzzles made with the vocabulary words.
6. Have students write and exchange a **cloze exercise** using the vocabulary words. A cloze exercise has a blank for each vocabulary word, and the surrounding context must clearly indicate which word belongs in each blank.

Each chapter analysis is organized into two basic elements: **Journal and Discussion Topics** and **Chapter Summary.** Introducing one or more of the Journal and Discussion Topics prior to reading will help focus students' reading of the chapter. Choose questions that will not give away important plot elements.

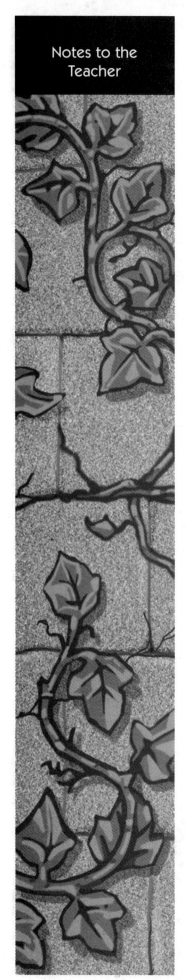

Journal and Discussion Topics

The **Journal and Discussion Topics** include directions for the students' **Reader Response Journals** and questions for **Discussion** to help the students become engaged with the literature. Students will benefit by reading with their journals beside them. This will allow them to easily note any unfamiliar vocabulary that was not presented to the class, questions they have about the literature, and their own reactions as they enter into the experience of the story. Journals can also be used for written dialogue between you and students. If you wish to do this, periodically collect the journals and respond to students' comments. It is important for students to know beforehand whether their journals are private or public. In either case, journals should not be corrected or graded but only recorded as being used. You may also wish to keep your own journal.

Discussion can take place between partners, in small groups, or within a whole class. Students may also wish to reflect on the discussion in their journals. Discussion starters include

1. A group retelling of the chapter in which everyone participates.
2. Each group member telling the most striking moment in the chapter for him or her.
3. Each group member sharing a question she or he would like to ask the author or a character about the chapter.
4. Each student telling what he or she liked most or least about the chapter.
5. A discussion of how the chapter relates to the preceding chapter and the rest of the book that preceded it.

Discussion can end with predictions about what will happen in the next chapter. Each student should note predictions in her or his journal.

Always ask students to retell (or summarize) the material. The retelling can be oral, artistic (for example, a storyboard), or prose. Retelling can take place in the discussion groups or in the journals.

Chapter Summary

The **Chapter Summary** for each chapter is included for teacher use. It provides an at-a-glance scan of the chapter events and should be used as a companion to the work of literature being studied, not instead of it. Use it to refresh your memory about the contents of each chapter.

The Groupings of Literature

We have among our titles a group of works that could be presented as part of a unit called "The Journey." We present groupings of literature so that you can easily present works as a unit. The works of literature resonate with each other, providing a multi-faceted look at a variety of **themes** such as

- The journey as a metaphor
- Coping with change
- Safety versus risk-taking
- Change is opportunity
  (a Chinese saying)
- Choices
- Trust
- Flexibility
- The journey versus the arrival
- Resourcefulness

Since no substantial work of literature has only a single theme, "The Journey" is not the only possible grouping for the works of literature. But references to themes can both help focus students' attention as they read and help them link works of literature together in meaningful ways. A grouping of books

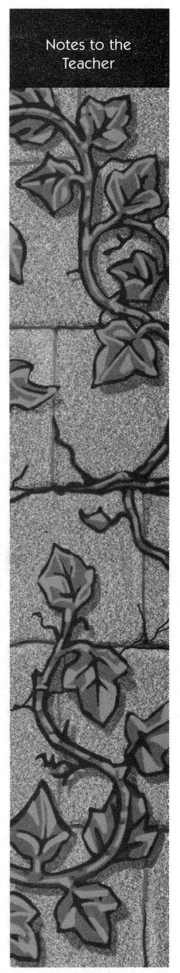

can also throw light on **Big Ideas.** Big Ideas worth considering include the following:

- How does context (cultural, social, etc.) affect us?
- How can personal desire be balanced with other responsibilities?
- What kinds of circumstances lead to personal development and growth?
- How is place important in our lives? What kinds of changes can occur when we change our location?

OTHER FEATURES OF THE CHALLENGING LEVEL

Strategy Pages

Strategy Pages throughout the series have been developed to increase students' understanding of strategies they can use to enhance their understanding of literature. Some important examples are

- Monitoring (such as adjusting reading rate; using context, including illustrations, to clarify meaning; rereading)
- Identifying important information (such as marking a text)
- Summarizing
- Evaluating
- Understanding the tools that writers use to make meaning—the elements of literature such as theme, plot, character, allusion, symbolism, metaphor.

The pages for each literature selection reinforce the strategies important for engaging deeply with that particular work of literature. You may copy and distribute these pages. Students can answer on the back of the page or on a separate sheet of paper.

Testing

At the end of each chapter grouping, a comprehensive open-book **Test** has been provided for your use. Each test includes vocabulary exercises and short essays. You may copy and distribute these pages.

An Answer Key is provided at the back of the book for each Test. Answers to essay questions are, of necessity, incomplete and only suggestive. Students' answers should be fully developed.

Writer's Forum

Suggestions for writing are presented under the **Writer's Forum** heading throughout this guide. You can choose from these suggestions or substitute your own creative-writing ideas.

Each Writer's Forum includes both instruction and directions for a particular writing task. Students will write in a variety of genres relating to the text and their own experience of the text. As you plan writing lessons, allow enough time for students to engage in the writing process:

- **Prewrite** (brainstorm and plan their work)
- **Draft** (give a shape to their ideas on paper)
- **Review** (revisit their work with an eye to improving it, on their own as well as with peers, with you, or with others)
- **Revise** (make changes that they feel will improve their draft)
- **Proofread** (check for accuracy in grammar, mechanics, and spelling)
- **Publish** (present their work to others in some way)

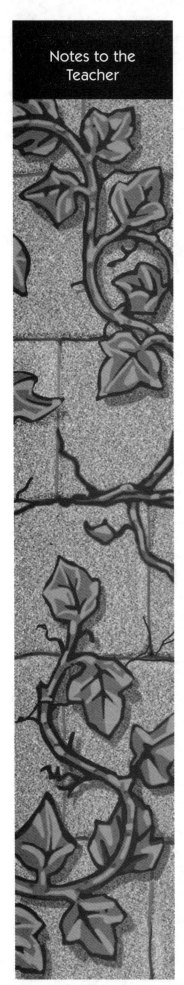

INTRODUCING THE LITERATURE

Students will be better prepared to become involved with the work of literature if they can place it in a context. The process of **contextualizing** a work of literature begins with accessing their **prior knowledge** about the book, the author, the genre, and the subject. A class discussion is a good forum for this to take place. After you have found out what, if any, familiarity students have with the book and author and what they have been able to discern about the genre and subject, you can provide any necessary background knowledge and, if it seems appropriate, correct any misapprehensions students have. See **Strategy 1: Beginning a Book,** pages 12–13.

Explain that in a work of fiction, an author creates an imaginary world. An important task in beginning a literature selection is to come to terms with that world. Point out that it is possible to consciously assess one's own understanding of literature and that this process is called **metacognitive reflection.** You may wish to model this process using a **think-aloud** approach as you go through the material on pages 12–13. To do this, simply read aloud the portion of *Redwall* needed to answer the questions, and speak aloud your thoughts as you formulate your responses, making explicit the connections and prior knowledge you are developing in your thoughts.

After students have a beginning notion of the context of a work, you can proceed with the prereading activities that students will do prior to reading every chapter.

Sample Lesson Plan

Engaging **Prereading** activities include the following:

- Preview vocabulary and do a vocabulary exercise.
- Review the events of the previous chapter.
- Based on what they already know, have students examine their expectations about what will happen next, but be ready for surprises. Have students consider the chapter title and any illustrations. Use appropriate questions from page 13 or a prediction guide. Students can fill in the guide as a class, in groups, or individually. Encourage students to continue using this kind of self-questioning in their Reader Response Journals.

During Reading, students read with their Reader Response Journals. (You may wish to give them some of the journal and discussion topics before they read, or after they have read a particular portion of the book.) Additional journal activities they can use with every chapter include the following:

- A summary of the events of the chapter
- Evaluations of the characters and/or text
- Questions about what they have read
- Associations they have made between the text and other texts, experiences, or situations
- Notes on the images the text evoked
- Notes on the feelings the text evoked

After Reading, students complete the Journal and Discussion Topics, the Writer's Forum and Strategy Pages (if any), and the Test.

Bibliography

As you and your students immerse yourselves in this work of literature, you may wish to consult other works by the same author, thematically related works, video and/or audio productions of the work, and criticism. Here is a brief list of works that may be useful:

Adams, Richard. *Watership Down.*

Alexander, Lloyd. *The Arkadians.*

Alexander, Lloyd. *The Book of Three.*

Cooper, Susan. *Over Sea, Under Stone.*

Homer. *The Odyssey.* (many translations available)

Jacques, Brian. *Mossflower.*

_____. *Mattimeo.*

_____. *Mariel of Redwall.*

_____. *Salamandastron.*

_____. *Martin the Warrior.*

_____. *The Bellmaker.*

_____. *The Long Patrol.*

_____. *The Outcast of Redwall.*

_____. *Pearls of Lutra.*

_____. *Pearls of Lutra* and *The Long Patrol—audio recording (Putnam Audio).*

_____. *Redwall—*audio recording: complete and unabridged. (Listening Library)

Le Guin, Ursula. *A Wizard of Earthsea.*

Tolkien, J. R. R. *The Annotated Hobbit.*

White, T.H. *The Sword in the Stone.*

Notes: You may wish to inform students that some British slang is used in this book, primarily by Basil. The sparrows speak pidgin English (imagine the pun intended), the moles speak a lower-class dialect that is best understood by saying their words aloud. Both the sparrows' and the moles' pronunciation is represented through spelling changes.

The illustrations vary, depending on the edition. The hardcover and older Avon paperback have a header illustration at the top of each chapter. The Berkley edition does not. The maps and covers also differ. All page references throughout are for the Berkley edition.

Poem & Introduction

nought	xiv	nothing
twixt	xiv	between; amid
threshold	xiv	doorway; boundary
wield	xiv	use effectively
languishing	xv	fading
tinted	xv	lightly colored; stained
heralded	xv	announced; foreshadowed
foursquare	xv	having the shape of a square
flanked	xv	bordered
Abbey	xv	a monastery ruled by an Abbot
undulating	xv	rising and falling like the waves
dusky	xv	dark colored
mantle	xv	cloak; cape
quarried	xv	dug up
hue	xv	color

1-1

cloisters	3	covered walks found in monasteries
novice	3	one who is in a probationary period in a religious order
cowl	3	a hooded cloak like that of a monk
Abbot	3	the head of a monastery
buffoon	3	clown
singed	3	burned
humility	4	meekness; humbleness; modesty
yearnings	4	desires; cravings
gnarled	4	knotted; twisted
sedate	4	calm and dignified
clad	4	dressed
garbed	4	attired
conversed	4	talked; discussed
feigning	4	pretending; affecting
lest	4	in case
jauntily	4	in a lively manner
nonchalantly	4	casually; without a care
shafts	4	beams; rays
dust-motes	4	dust-particles; dust-specks
tapestry	4	woven cloth (often containing pictures)
chronicle	4	historical record
vermin	5	small harmful animals
forsook	5	gave up; abandoned
vocation	5	calling to a particular course of life: the religious life or marriage or being single
impoverished	5	poor; destitute
predators	5	those who kill other animals for food
solemnity	6	seriousness; austerity
bidden	6	told; ordered
sticklebacks	6	scaleless, bony fish
bobbed	6	nodded
superior	6	the head of a religious house, e.g., an abbot
benignly	6	kindly; gently
Almoner	6	one who gives money or food to the poor

1-2

Scourge	7	one who inflicts pain or punishment
pike	7	large freshwater fish
bilge	7	the lowest part of a ship's hull
rodent	7	small gnawing mammals
graven	8	carved

1-3

sconces	9	candle holders
angling	9	fishing
Jubilee	9	a special anniversary (usually the fiftieth)
amid	9	in the middle of
culinary	9	having to do with the preparation of food
Friar	9	brother in a religious order
ranting	10	talking excitedly
delirious	10	overflowing with excitement
epic	10	beyond the ordinary
cordial	10	stimulating drink
rickets	10	skeletal disease caused by lack of sunlight and/or Vitamin D
gyrated	11	spun around; revolved
cavorting	11	prancing; capering
sultana	11	raisin
legerdemain	11	slight of the hand; magic
awestruck	11	amazed; dumbfounded
belfry	11	bell tower
reverently	11	worshipfully; respectfully
encompassing	12	surrounding; enveloping
tubers	12	edible underground stems, e.g., potatoes
devilled	12	highly seasoned, often by mustard/cayenne
purée	12	soft dish made from ground vegetables
marinated	12	soaked in a sauce to enrich the flavor
steeped	12	stewed
aromatic	12	fragrant
swagger	12	strut
ungainly	12	clumsy; awkward
pompous	12	self-important
Milord	12	address to Englishman of noble rank
pièce de résistance	12	the chief dish of a feast
culprit	12	guilty one
sniggers	12	rude laughs; snickers
precariously	13	insecurely

1-4

mutiny	14	rebellion; uprising
insubordination	14	disobedience
flay	14	skin
mangy	14	tattered; scruffy
haunches	15	hindquarters; hind legs
juggernaut	15	huge being that crushes what's in its way
ebbing	15	flowing out; vanishing
visage	15	face; countenance

1-5

slackened off	16	let up; lessened
replete	16	filled to the brim
specter	16	something disturbing or haunting
charitable	16	given to the poor or those in need
bidding	16	request
temperaments	16	characters
clambered	16	climbed; scrambled
tittered	17	giggled
slandering	17	lying
trundled	18	pulled; rolled
ambled	18	sauntered; strolled
nocturnal	18	awake and active at night
balmy	18	pleasant; mild; warm
rambler	18	climbing rose
dormant	18	not blooming
slumber	19	sleep
cutlasses	19	short curved swords
slunk	19	crept
rearguard	20	protection in back of the group

1-6

bolting	21	running out of control
blinkered	21	wearing blinders
careered	21	ran at full speed
reins	21	straps connected to bit in horse's mouth, used to control it
tracers	21	straps connecting a horse to the vehicle it pulls (American: traces)
contemptuously	21	derisively; haughtily
skittles	21	pins used in bowling games
tripes	22	worthless things (a curse)
cock your lugs up	22	tilt your ears up (slang)
berth	22	place to sleep
forage	22	scavenge; scrounge

1-7

infested	23	overrun; swarming
speculation	24	guessing about the future
fractious	24	fretful; irritable
bogey	25	spook
abashed	25	ashamed; sheepish
ninnies	25	blockheads; dolts
ferocity	25	viciousness; brutality
migratory	26	changing location seasonally
garrulous	26	talkative
undermined	27	eroded; tore away
shoring	27	a system of supports or props
hordes	27	troops; swarms; mobs
consternation	27	alarm; dismay; agitation
mite	27	a very small creature
puling	27	whining
brandishing	27	waving a weapon in a threatening way

1-8

allotted	28	given as a share or a portion
shrouded	28	enveloped; concealed
phantom	28	ghostly; like a specter
relish	28	enjoy the idea of
carnage	28	butchery; bloodshed
desolation	28	bleakness; devastation
wreaked	28	caused something (destructive)
pursuer	28	one who chases and tries to capture
leaden	29	heavy; burdensome
avenging	29	paying back for misdeeds
scavengers	29	foragers; searchers
baleful	29	threatening
paltry	29	meager; insignificant
carcass	29	corpse; remains
spit	30	skewer
recruits	30	trainees newly added to an organization
press-ganged	30	pressured by a group empowered to use violence to get recruits for the military
nomads	30	wanderers
impassively	30	unemotionally
scurvy	30	vile
buckoes	30	young fellows; lads
motley	31	mixed; sundry
implements	31	tools; equipment

1-9

meandered	32	wandered without direction
refuge	32	safety; sanctuary
diligent	32	hard working; industrious
abundance	32	plenty; bounty
bilberry	32	a sweet fruit resembling the blueberry
hovering	33	hanging
haven	33	refuge; shelter
assessed	33	considered
beauteous	33	full of beauty; lovely
abode	33	home; dwelling
tinged	33	affected
fret	33	worry; be vexed
forestalled	33	hindered; prevented
disillusion	33	to dash hopes
sanctuary	33	safety; shelter
makeshift	33	temporary
stolidly	33	unemotionally; stoically
render	34	give
glib	35	artful; slick
competent	35	capable; skilled
abusive	35	rude; insulting
upstart	36	someone who has gained power suddenly and unexpectedly
condescending	36	patronizing; superior
brazen	36	describing the sound of brass being struck
construing	36	explaining
allies	36	supporters; partners
camouflage	37	hidden; concealed
scaled	37	climbed; surmounted
instinctively	37	naturally; innately
formidable	37	overwhelming; staggering
deterrent	37	drawback; hindrance
hackles	37	hair on the neck and back of an animal
ramparts	37	barriers; fortifications

1-10

ploy	38	tactic; stratagem
berserk	38	in an uncontrollable frenzy
begone	39	leave; get out of here
derision	39	scorn; contempt
masonry	39	stonework
parapet	39	low wall around the edge of a roof
visor	39	the movable front piece of a helmet
bumpkin	39	someone awkward and unsophisticated
mirthlessly	40	without joy
ponderously	40	heavily
bristling	40	similar in appearance to a bristly brush
staves	40	poles
menacing	40	threatening
emanating	41	radiating; giving off
enslaved	41	imprisoned
insolently	41	disrespectfully; insultingly
restraining	42	restrictive; limiting
intervention	42	interruption; interference
muster	43	summon
cringed	43	flinched; winced
impudence	43	impertinence; insolence
transfixed	43	frozen; unable to move
deputizing	44	acting as a substitute; taking command
livid	44	furious; enraged

STRATEGY 1 Beginning a Book

Directions: Read the explanation, then answer the questions.

When an artist or craftworker sets about creating a work, there is a set of standard tools, techniques, and products available. The sculptor, for example, has chisels of various shapes and sizes, saws of various descriptions, and a choice of clay, metal, marble, wood, etc. The product may be a relief, a statue, or a collage. And the techniques used may include whittling, welding, carving, or throwing on the potter's wheel. In addition, there are certain conventions, such as perspective, that the sculptor may choose to employ or not. The sculptor does not use every technique and material in every work, and the sculptor's choices are guided by the sculptor's goal, which might be the answer to a question such as, "How can I effectively communicate my vision?" The viewer coming to see the finished product can see it all at one time (or, if it is a large statue, within a few seconds by moving around it). Moving closer and further away, attending to detail, shape, color, texture, and the effect of the whole, the viewer can come to understand the sculptor.

The writer is an artist who works in words, and these words create images, thoughts, and feelings in the reader. Like the sculptor, the writer usually isn't there when the reader experiences the product (in this case a book), but reading is, nevertheless, an act of communication. Like the painter, the writer works to communicate a vision to people who are not present with him or her. The reader's understanding of the standard tools, techniques, products, and conventions of the writer help the reader to understand the vision. But at the same time that we try to understand the writer's communication, we must acknowledge that each reader also brings an individual and unique understanding to the act of reading, and so no 2 readers will experience a book in exactly the same way. Different readers will have different insights and feelings, so discussion between and among readers can enrich the experience of all.

Beginning a book is particularly important, because readers starting a book are entering a new and uncharted territory. When you are starting a book, paying particular attention to the writer's use of tools, techniques, and conventions can help.

TITLE: It is a convention for a novel to have a title, found on the front cover, the spine, and the title page. The title of the book may explicitly tell what the book is about, may hint about the story, or may seem very mysterious. Depending on the title, you may feel interested, curious, hopeful, etc. If you know anything about the author already, for example, that Jacques worked as a comedian, it might help you make predictions about the content of the book.

COVER ILLUSTRATION: Most books have a picture on the cover. The writer may or may not have had a voice in what appears, so the illustration may not represent the writer's vision. Nevertheless, it can give you some idea of characters, setting, and plot in the story.

COPYRIGHT PAGE: The copyright page tells the dates of the book's publication. It can help you know whether the book is recent or older.

OTHER BOOKS BY: Sometimes there is a list before the title page that names other books by the same author. If you are familiar with any of these other works, you may have some idea of what is to come. This is also true if you have heard about the book from friends, read a book review, heard the book on audiotape, or seen a movie version. This is some of your prior knowledge about the book.

TABLE OF CONTENTS: While some books have unnamed divisions, sometimes authors title their chapters or sections. Like the book title, these titles may reveal more or less about what happens in the book.

INSIDE ILLUSTRATIONS: Some books are illustrated throughout with drawings, paintings, photographs, etc. There is a map at the beginning of *Redwall* as well as a picture at the head of each chapter in the book. See page 14 for more information about these illustrations.

BACK COVER BLURB: The note on the back cover is advertising, meant to give away enough of the story to pique your interest and convince you to buy the book. It doesn't necessarily reflect the writer's vision, or the most meaningful view of the story. In addition, it often tells you about an important part in the middle of the story, and you may prefer not to know this in advance.

FIRST FEW PARAGRAPHS: The first few paragraphs of the story provide the writer with the first opportunity to introduce the characters, plot, setting, and theme of the story. Read carefully to learn as much as you can about the world of the book. In addition, Jacques has provided a poem and a 3-paragraph introduction before the first chapter.

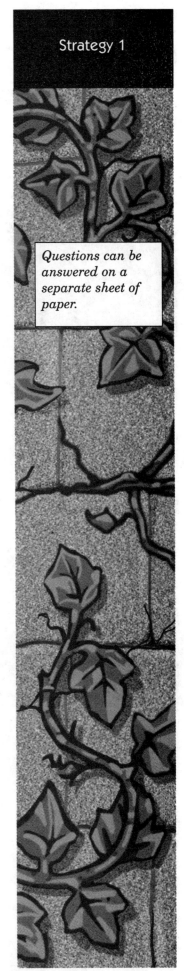

Questions can be answered on a separate sheet of paper.

1. What is your reaction to the title of the book?

2. Describe the cover illustration. What can you gather from it?

3. Based on the title and the cover, what do you think this book will be about?

4. How long has it been since this book was first published?

5. What, if anything, do you already know about Jacques, his works, or *Redwall*?

6. What can you tell about the story from the section titles and illustrations?

7. What do the poem and three introductory paragraphs tell you?

8. Read page 3 and the first 3 complete paragraphs on 4. Who seem(s) to be the most important character(s)? How can you tell?

9. What is the narrator like? Can you trust the narrator's perceptions? How did you decide?

10. Finish Chapter 1. Where does the story take place? Is it a real setting or a setting created by the author? What special characteristics does the setting have?

11. What clues are there to the genre of this story?

12. What does the theme or focus of the story seem to be?

13. What do you predict will happen next in the story?

14. What more do you want to know about the setting and the characters?

STRATEGY 2   Maps and Illustrations

Directions: Read the explanation, then answer the questions.

A **map** is a flat representation of part or all of the real world or an imaginary world. A number of journey stories have maps to help the reader become acquainted with the geography of the world of the story. Some of the elements found on most maps and included on the map on pages viii–ix of *Redwall* include

- **Title:** Maps can be labeled with a title that identifies the location.
- **Compass Rose:** A compass rose identifies the cardinal directions (north, south, east, and west) with respect to the layout of the map. Most modern maps have north at the top.
- **Symbols:** Most maps have a legend that identifies the symbols. This map uses symbols that we are expected to recognize without aid.
- **Distance and Size:** Jacques does not provide a bar scale to indicate distances. We can still assume that for A, B, and C on the map, if C is twice as far from A as B is from A, this relationship mirrors the relationship in the world of Redwall Abbey.
- **Labels:** There are labels for important places.

1. What symbols are on the map?

2. What animals do you see on the map? What do you think their presence indicates?

This section applies to the hardcover book and the Avon paperback:

Each of the 58 chapters in this book is headed by an **illustration** that gives a clue to the chapter contents. The illustrations show characters, events, settings, important or symbolic objects, and occasionally words.

3. For each chapter, note what is shown in the illustration. When you have finished, make some predictions about the contents of the story.

Book One

Chapter 1

Journal and Discussion Topics

1. How does Jacques provide a context in which to review the background information on Redwall Abbey that readers need?
2. Describe the Abbey's mission in your own words.
3. What does Matthias want? Do you think he's likely to get it? Why or why not?
4. Do you think it is likely that Matthias could be like Martin? Why or why not?
5. How does the Abbot's attitude toward Matthias evolve through the chapter?

Summary

Young Matthias, a novice in the Abbey of Redwall, is pausing in his duties to gaze at the sky, when he trips and falls, dropping a basket of nuts and tumbling to a stop right in front of Abbot Mortimer. As they walk together at Mortimer's suggestion, the Father Abbot notices Matthias gazing with admiration at the portion of the famous Redwall tapestry that portrays Martin the Warrior. The Abbot takes the opportunity to explain the mission of the Abbey as a peaceful place of sanctuary and healing. He explains to Matthias that the day of the warrior is past and that Matthias's vocation consists in obedience, not victorious battles. He then sends Matthias on a mission to catch a fish for the Redwall feast planned for that evening.

Chapter 2

Journal and Discussion Topics

1. Compare and contrast the illustration for this chapter with the verbal description. (Use only with hardcover or Avon edition.)
2. Draw a picture of Cluny based on the verbal description.
3. What does the narrator's explicit reference to Cluny being "evil" suggest to you about what will happen in the book?
4. The narrator indicates that Cluny doesn't care where he ends up. Where do you predict he will go?
5. In what ways do you think Cluny might be similar to a "God of War" (page 8)?
6. What do you think the arrival of Cluny the Scourge and his army in the neighborhood will mean for the Abbey? For Matthias?
7. What might happen to the horse, cart, and 500 rats?

Summary

The scene shifts to Cluny the Scourge, a rat who, along with his army of 500 followers (who are linked to Cluny by fear rather than loyalty), is riding on a hay wagon pulled by a runaway horse who plunges ahead, terrified by its horrid cargo. Cluny does not care where the wagon goes, but, as it happens, they are within 15 miles of Redwall Abbey.

STRATEGY 3

*Directions:
Read the expla-
nation, then
answer the ques-
tions.*

Fantasy is fiction that has some elements in common with fairy tales, some elements in common with epic, and other elements in common with science fiction. Fantasy and science fiction are genres that incorporate elements that are not real. They may both use magic, imaginary creatures, and imaginary settings. Fantasy and epic can both focus on the adventures or journey of a hero who overcomes great odds, and both can incorporate elements of mythology, including gods and goddesses.

Here are some of the elements that *Redwall* shares with other fantasy stories:

- good and evil
- a sword
- a puzzle to solve
- a quest
- a wise older guide
- emphasis on food and fellowship
- a snake
- the theft of a sacred object

In animal fantasies, our irrational feelings that certain animals are "good" or "bad" (appealing or unappealing to us) are often reinforced by the author's choice of which animals portray evil characters and which portray good characters. Although the animal characters are human in many ways, their animal characteristics allow them to perform deeds that are beyond the scope of human powers.

1. As you read, keep a list of the species of animals that are "good" and those that are "evil." Do they fit with your feelings about these animals?

2. As you read, make note of feats the animals perform that humans could not.

Proper Names

Character names (and place names) can be symbolic or descriptive. The introduction on page xv explaining the origin of the name "Redwall" confirms that in this story, readers can expect names to have a meaning beyond simple identification. In addition, most of the "good" animals have human names, while the rats are given names that make them harder to identify with. Sometimes the meaning of a name may be a simple pleasant or unpleasant association. The name of the rat "Scumnose" is an example of an unpleasant association, as are most of the other rat names. "Cornflower" is an example of a pleasant association. The name "Matthias," on the other hand, has a deeper meaning. It is the name of the man chosen to replace the apostle Judas who betrayed Christ. Little is known about him except that he filled the place of another. "Methuselah" is an Old Testament figure who lived for a very long time. Asmodeas (pronounced as-mo-DE-us) is an evil spirit, king of the demons in Jewish demonology.

3. Categorize the names by how you can make meaning from them.

Chapter 3

Journal and Discussion Topics
1. What exploit helps Matthias gain recognition in this chapter? What kinds of recognition does he receive?
2. Give 4 examples of Abbey etiquette (good manners) that are followed at the feast.
3. The Abbot asks Friar Hugo about the food stores at the Abbey because he wants to make sure that all the Jubilee guests have enough to eat. Why might Jacques have considered this important background information for the reader?
4. How does Matthias feel about Cornflower? How do you know?

Summary
Following the Abbot's request, Matthias goes with Brother Alf to catch a fish, and they hook a 2-pound grayling, which Friar Hugo prepares. Guests arrive for the Abbott's Jubilee with gifts and the Abbot, concerned that they might run out of food, consults with Friar Hugo, who assures him that the storehouses are full of a variety of foodstuffs. After a period of entertainment by 3 otters and Ambrose Spike (the hedgehog), the Abbot says grace, and the feast begins. Matthias, sitting by Cornflower Fieldmouse, is divided between taking care of 2 baby Churchmice and admiring Cornflower. The Abbot samples the grayling and pronounces it "exquisite."

Chapter 4

Journal and Discussion Topics
1. What do Skullface's reaction to Cluny and Cluny's treatment of Skullface suggest to you about how Cluny's army works?
2. How is Cluny deciding where he's going?
3. Predict what will happen in the story, given the indications you've received in the first 4 chapters.

Summary
When the horse stops pulling the hay cart because it is exhausted, Cluny orders Skullface to bite it. When Skullface protests, Cluny whips him into submission. Skullface leaps onto the horse's back, and the terrified animal takes off without waiting to be bitten. Skullface, unprepared for the sudden leap forward, falls under the cart wheels, and Cluny sneers as Skullface dies.

Chapter 5

Journal and Discussion Topics

1. What does the Abbot arrange for the Churchmouse family?
2. How does the relationship between Matthias and Cornflower develop? What difficulty could this relationship cause for Matthias?
3. What might be the significance of the rose failing to flower as usual?
4. Why does Constance decide to return to the Abbey?
5. Speculate on the consequences if the Abbot had not arranged the ride home for the two mice families?

Summary

The Abbot, who has arranged for food to be surreptitiously delivered to the Churchmice, commissions Matthias and Constance Badger to take the Churchmouse family home. Since Cornflower's family lives nearby, the Fieldmice go along too. Cornflower, falling asleep with her head on Matthias's shoulder, thinks about the significance of the Abbey rose not yet blooming this summer. Everyone dozes until they are startled into wakefulness by the passing of Cluny's cart pulled by the frantic horse. Constance pulls off the road in time to save them from a collision, and makes the decision to turn back to the Abbey in order to warn the Abbot. Matthias takes up a position of rearguard, as Constance turns the cart and heads back to Redwall.

Chapter 6

Journal and Discussion Topics

1. What character traits of Cluny are revealed by his response to the accident with the cart?
2. What indications are there in this chapter that Cluny will be heading for Redwall Abbey?
3. How does Cluny plan to get information about the local situation?
4. What elements of the Church of St. Ninian does Cluny appreciate? Why?
5. What can you infer from the narrator's final comment in the chapter?
6. Contrast the caption of this chapter's illustration with the prayer of the Abbot on page 12.

Summary

Running aimlessly, the horse pulls the cart into 2 gateposts where it smashes, freeing the horse to run away, but killing and maiming many of the rat passengers. Cluny, showing no compassion, starts giving orders. He sends out scouts to find a classier lodging than the Church of St. Ninian where they have landed, suggesting the "big place on the way"—Redwall Abbey. He then sends a group of rats in search of recruits—rats, weasels, stoats, and ferrets, who can provide information about the local scene. He tells his followers to kill anyone who won't join. Finally, he sends some rats to find supplies and others to find any materials in the church or the churchyard that can be used as weapons.

STRATEGY 4   Setting: Redwall Abbey

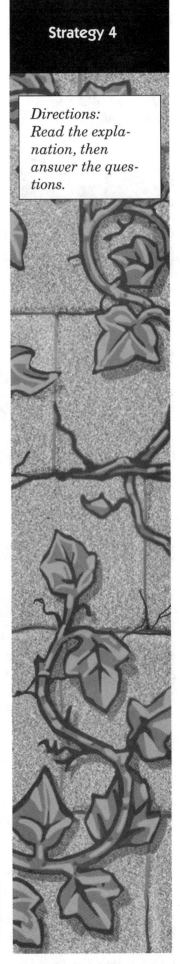

Directions: Read the explanation, then answer the questions.

Setting is both the world in which the story takes place and the changing scenery that serves as the backdrop for each scene or chapter. Setting includes what the characters can see, hear, smell, and touch in their environment. Sights include

- Time of day
- Season of the year
- Plants and animals
- Natural features
- Weather
- Landscape
- Buildings or other structures

The general setting of this story is Mossflower country, a land with certain kinds of inhabitants, certain kinds of landscape, certain plants and animals and weather, certain rules and customs. The particular setting within Mossflower country changes little from scene to scene and chapter to chapter—most of the action is located in and around Redwall Abbey, St. Ninian's Church, and Mossflower Woods.

Setting can serve different functions in different stories, and at different times in the same story. It may be a mere backdrop to the story, or it may have a more integral part. The setting may be symbolic and be a source of information about the inhabitants of the area. The setting may create conflicts for the characters of the story. The setting may help or hinder the characters in achieving their goal. It may provide materials or resources that help the characters solve problems, or create physical hardships or challenges that are difficult to overcome. Setting also helps establish characterization. For example, from reading the account of Cluny sending his henchrats to find items in the church that can be used as weapons, you can get a sense of Cluny's willingness to violate even the most sacred things for his own ends.

Although a novel is classified as a narrative, that is, a type of writing that tells a story, sections of a novel that deal with the setting are usually passages of description. Because most of the story of *Redwall* is set in Redwall Abbey, it is important to pay attention to the names and descriptions of the locations there. You may even wish to construct your own map to help you understand the spatial relationships of the various locales. Already, you have heard about

- the cloisters
- Cavern Hole
- cellars
- the Great Hall
- the Abbey kitchen
- the Abbey belfry

As you notice the setting, try to figure out what the writer is trying to convey. Pay attention to the possibilities and problems created by the setting in order to take advantage of hints the writer is giving about what might happen next.

Extend the following chart to create a record of Redwall settings and their functions.

Page #	Setting Description	Function(s) in Story

Book One
Chapter 7, Page 23
Chapter 8, Page 28

mossflower woods

quarry

the abbey

st. ninian's church

Chapter 7

Journal and Discussion Topics

1. What does the illustration for this chapter convey to you? (Use only with hardcover or Avon edition.)
2. What kinds of evidence are considered important by the Redwall council?
3. What are Methuselah's gifts?
4. What deeds are attributed to Cluny and his followers?
5. Why do some of the participants at first dismiss the possibility that Cluny is a real threat?
6. What do you think Matthias means by being "ready"? If you were at Redwall, what preparations would you make?
7. How does the coming of Cluny make Matthias's dream a possibility?

Summary

Matthias and Constance present their story to the Council of Elders at Redwall and answer the questions that the Council members set. Through the Abbot's questioning of Matthias, the identity of the rat leader becomes clear to the Abbot—the horde of hundreds of rats is being led by the infamous Cluny the Scourge. But the Council does not accept this—they believe that Cluny is a legend, made up by parents to scare their children into good behavior. After Constance chastises them for lack of faith in the Abbot's assessment, the Abbot calls for Methuselah, the Abbey historian, who recounts the history of Cluny's slow encroachment into their region. Convinced by Methuselah, the Council becomes terrified. It is Matthias who suggests their course of action—to prepare for the arrival of Cluny—and the Abbot seconds it.

Chapter 8

Journal and Discussion Topics

1. Whom do you think is pictured in the illustration for this chapter? Why? (Use only with hardcover or Avon edition.)
2. After reading about Cluny's dream, whom do you think the illustration depicts? (Use only with hardcover or Avon edition.)
3. How does Cluny toy with his followers?
4. Assess Cluny's leadership techniques, given the treatment of the new recruits.

Summary

Cluny, dreaming pleasantly of destroying everything in his path, is disturbed by the appearance in his dream of a phantom figure, a mouse in a hooded robe, wielding a sword and chasing Cluny, who for the first time in his life, runs away. Just as the mouse, now grown to giant stature, is about to strike a death blow, Cluny is awakened by the Joseph Bell. Cluny is not sure whether or not to take his dream as an omen. His thoughts are interrupted by the arrival of 2 scavengers with the paltry results of their search for food. After pretending to be pleased, Cluny assaults them and sends them out again. The recruiters have succeeded better, using threats and force, and many join Cluny's army, willingly or unwillingly. Cluny has the articles of service recited to them, and suddenly attacks them. When they run from him, he laughs and tells them that their use to him is that they will die in his battles. They raise their weapons and salute him, calling out his name, "Cluny, Cluny, Cluny the Scourge!"

STRATEGY 5

Plot Conflict

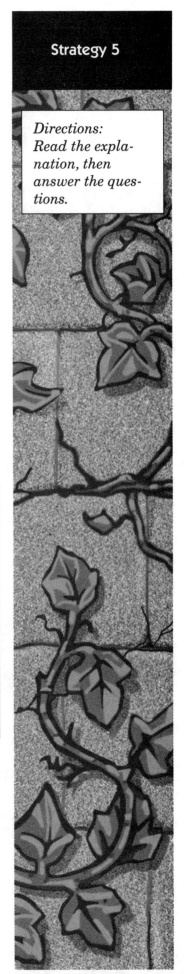

Directions: Read the explanation, then answer the questions.

Conflict is the core of a story's plot. Conflict is what makes us wonder if the protagonist will attain his or her goal. Conflict is what adds suspense and excitement to stories. Usually there is one overarching conflict that takes up much of the book. But each chapter or scene in the book usually also has conflict on a smaller scale.

The struggles that a protagonist undergoes in a story can be either **internal** or **external.** In an **internal** conflict, the protagonist undergoes an interior struggle. He or she might have conflicting desires, values, personality traits, and/or motives. People often have internal conflicts as they grow and develop from one stage in their lives to the next. An internal conflict takes place in the character's mind and heart.

In an **external** conflict, the protagonist struggles with something or someone outside of himself or herself. The conflict may be with another individual, with a task or problem, with society, with nature, with an idea, or with a force, such as good or evil.

1. What appear to be the overarching conflicts in this story? Cite evidence to support your conclusion.

2. Extend and fill in the chart to show how most chapters contain a mini-plot with a conflict and a resolution.

CHAPTER	CONFLICT AND RESOLUTION
1	
2	
3	
4	
5	
6	
7	
8	
9	
10	

3. Another element of chapter organization in this story of a war between good and evil is which army each particular chapter focuses on. Keep track of how Jacques shifts back and forth by marking C for Cluny and Company or M for Matthias and Mice (or both) by the chapter number in your chart.

STRATEGY 6 Point of View

Directions:
Read the explanation, then answer the questions.

A story is always told by someone. This person is called the narrator. The narrator may be someone who participates in the action of the story or someone outside the action of the story. The narrator may have a limited range of knowledge, or may know everything there is to know about the story. The narrator may be reliable or unreliable. All of these factors go into what is called the story's **point of view.**

Stories can be told in the **first-person point of view**. In this case, the narrator is usually someone who was present or involved in the action of the story, and this person tells the story using the pronoun *I* to indicate personal involvement.

Stories can also be told in the **second-person point of view,** which is distinguished by the fact that the narrator speaks to the reader as *you,* and addresses the reader directly, as if they were speaking together.

The **third-person point of view** is the point of view of a narrator who is separate from the action and tells it from a greater distance than a first-person narrator would.

A narrator can be **omniscient,** knowing all the action of the story even including what is going on in all the characters' minds and knowing what will happen before it happens, or **limited** to knowledge of the perspective of only one character.

It is an essential point that the reader cannot assume that the narrator of the story is the author. Usually the narrator of a work of fiction is a persona created by the author for the purpose of conveying the story.

1. Find 3 passages that show the narrator's access to a variety of characters' inner thoughts and feelings.

2. What seems to be the narrator's relationship to the events of the story?

Chapter 9

Journal and Discussion Topics

1. Compare and contrast the Abbot's and Constance's expectations for the future of the Abbey.
2. Does Matthias have the potential to become more like Martin? Explain.
3. On page 36 is a list of the animals seeking sanctuary at Redwall. Compare it to those who joined Cluny (page 30). What do you think of the way Jacques has allotted the animals to the sides of good and evil?
4. John Churchmouse announces that he can see Cluny's army approaching. What expectations do you have for the initial confrontation?

Summary

The Abbot and Constance walk through the Abbey grounds together, enjoying the peace of the Abbey. The Abbot expresses his belief that a miracle will save Redwall from tragedy, and Constance thinks, but does not say, that the days of fabled deeds are past. In the meantime, Methuselah, able to read Matthias's thoughts, encourages him to imitate Martin, whom he already resembles in some significant ways. Methuselah notes Martin's youth, his impulsiveness, his innocence, and his gift of leadership. The mice at the gate report that a rat tried to gain entrance to have an injury treated, and when they voiced their suspicions, he threatened them and ran off. While some of the creatures react emotionally, Matthias reacts practically, suggesting that other creatures in the area be warned and that a guard be mounted on the wall. Brother Methuselah, capable of speaking the language of all creatures, greets them all in the Abbot's name as they arrive at Redwall. Meanwhile, Constance and Matthias, mounting guard on the wall, hear the animals outside the Abbey go quiet and realize that Cluny is approaching.

Chapter 10

Journal and Discussion Topics

1. List the strategies that Cluny uses or is said to have at his disposal.
2. Do you think Cluny's assessment of the Redwall mice—"they'd sooner die than break their word to anyone"—is correct? Tell why or why not.
3. What strategic errors are committed in this chapter, in your opinion?
4. What do you infer from Cluny's dislike of honeyed milk?
5. What do you think of Cluny's dream, now that you know that Cluny has identified Martin the Warrior as the phantom mouse?

Summary

Having lost the element of surprise, Cluny plans a show of force. He is admitted to the Abbey for an audience with the Abbot, after the mice make sure he and his first in command, Redtooth, are unarmed. Matthias is dismayed because Cluny has realized that the defenders of the Abbey are untrained. In the Abbot's presence, Cluny has Redtooth begin to read articles of surrender, but Matthias interrupts by ripping the articles with his staff. As Redtooth prepares to attack Matthias, Constance knocks him over, and only the Abbot's intervention stops her from killing Redtooth. Cluny gives the Abbot till the following day to answer the demand for surrender, but the Abbot immediately and unequivocally states that they will never surrender. As he leaves, Cluny spots the same part of the Redwall tapestry that Matthias admired. Cluny recognizes Martin the Warrior as the mouse who appeared in his nightmare. As Cluny and Redtooth leave, Constance challenges Redtooth to single combat the next time they meet.

mossflower woods

quarry

the abbey

st. ninian's church

STRATEGY 7   Plot—The Design of a Story

The Freytag Pyramid

1. *Exposition*
2. *Complication or Rising Action*
3. *Climax or Crisis*
4. *Falling Action*
5. *Resolution or Denouement*

There are exciting stories and dull stories. There are westerns, adventure stories, mysteries, romances, thrillers, horror stories, science fiction stories, and fantasies. There are stories with happy endings and stories with sad endings. These differences can make stories seem worlds apart. But there is a common set of characteristics that almost all stories have—whether they are long or short, for adults or young people—that make them stories.

Every story has a plot or sequence of actions, a setting or settings where the action takes place, a character or group of characters who take action, and a narrator who tells the story to the reader.

People who study literature have come up with several different ways of talking about plot. When people talk about stories with young children, they often refer to the beginning, the middle, and the end. This is not just a notion for young children. These 3 parts are the way screenwriters and television writers arrange their scripts. Dramatists, on the other hand, often work with a 5-act play. The 5 acts each represents an essential and sequential part of the drama. Narrative is also often presented in high school and college classes as having a 5-book structure as follows:

1. **Exposition:** introduction of essential background information, as well as characters, situations, and conflicts. Exposition may be found throughout a story, as well as at the beginning.

2. **Complication or Rising Action:** the beginning of the central conflict in the story.

3. **Crisis:** (sometimes called the **turning point**) usually the point at which the main character's action or choice determines the outcome of the conflict. Or, **Climax:** the high point of the action.

4. **Falling Action:** the time when all the pieces fall into place and the ending becomes inevitable.

5. **Resolution or Denouement:** the conflicts are resolved and the story is concluded.

So do we look at a story as having 5 books or 3 books? One way we can think about it is to see where the 5 Books fit into the beginning, middle, and end:

Beginning: Exposition
Middle: Complication, ends with the Crisis
End: Climax (the beginning of the end) and Resolution

Writers adapt the plot structure to a particular story. They decide how much exposition should be included and where, how many conflicts there are, what's told to the reader, and what is left for the reader to figure out.

1. As you read *Redwall*, pause at the end of each chapter, and identify for yourself where it fits in the plot structure. Place it on a Freytag Pyramid of your own. Note the places in the story where you find the beginning of each of the 5 books. Use the back of this page for your response. The shape of your pyramid may not exactly match the model in the margin.

STRATEGY 8

Foreshadowing and Flashback

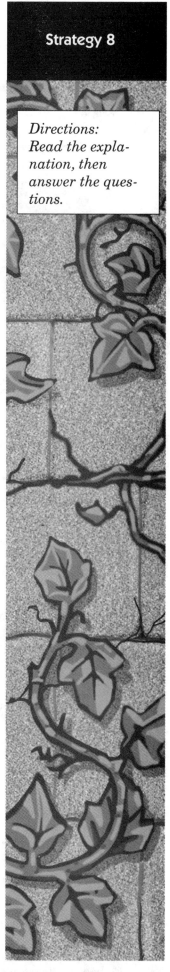

Directions: Read the explanation, then answer the questions.

Writers do not always tell plot events in chronological order. They may hint at events before their place in the sequence. This is called **foreshadowing,** and it lets readers know beforehand something about what is going to happen later. This technique helps create suspense and keeps the reader involved in the unfolding plot.

Foreshadowing may come from a character, from the setting, or from the narrator. For example, when we read about the Redwall signpost on the roadside (page 8), this element of the setting may suggest to us (along with our ideas of how good and evil come into contact in fantasies) that Cluny will attack Redwall. When we read a little farther and the narrator says, "Cluny was coming nearer!" we get further evidence to support our theory. If the cart is headed toward Redwall, then that's where he is coming nearer to, and we can expect a confrontation.

Writers may also go back to material that happened prior to the beginning of the story or earlier in the plot sequence. This is called **flashback.** Flashbacks give the reader necessary background material for understanding the story. Flashbacks may come from the narrator or the characters. When Abbot Mortimer, for example, begins his tale of Martin on page 5, "He arrived here in the deep winter when the Founders were under attack," this is a flashback. Flashback is part of the exposition in a novel. As you continue reading look for more examples of flashback.

1. Find 3 examples of foreshadowing. Are they from characters, the setting, or the narrator? What conclusions did you draw from them while you were reading?

Vocabulary

Look at each group of words. Tell why it is important in the story.

1. Abbot, Friar, Brother, Novice, Almoner, Sister

   _____

   _____

2. vermin, rodent, mangy, scavengers

   _____

   _____

3. sanctuary, haven, refuge

   _____

   _____

Essay Topics

1. Look back at the predictions you made about the book for Strategy 1 (page 13, question 13). Write a reflection on them based on what you know now. Make new predictions for the rest of the book.

2. Think of another story you know that features an animal listed on page 30 or 36 (rat, ferret, weasel, stoat, squirrel, mouse, vole, mole, or otter) that is personified (treated as a person). Compare and contrast the role of the creature in that story with its role in Redwall.

3. Pick a story that you think has a plot like Redwall so far. Explain the similarities you find.

4. What's your favorite moment in the story so far. Explain why.

5. Which character is your favorite? Tell why.

6. Rewrite a scene from the story, altering it by changing the point of view to one of the characters in the scene.

7. What do you think are Cluny's weak points?

8. In your opinion, what is one way in which Jacques could have improved something in Chapters 1–10?

1-11

tactician	46	one who understands and practices military strategy
curtailed	46	cut short
drag	46	slowing caused by friction
traction	46	power used to pull (something) forward
veritable	46	genuine; actual
loam	46	soil
trice	46	flash; twinkling
hillock	47	mound
rudimentary	47	basic; elementary
poultice	47	dressing for a wound
ruffian	47	tough guy; a bully
gullet	48	throat
deemed	48	reckoned; believed
daft	48	foolish; silly
jip	48	mild pain, usually from an old injury
emboldened	48	made brave; given courage
voluble	48	talkative
compassion	49	tenderness
indebted	50	grateful; obliged

1-12

pulpit	51	platform used for preaching
hassocks	51	footstools
choir loft	51	balcony from which a church choir sings
lady chapel	51	chapel dedicated to The Virgin Mary (Our Lady)
lectern	51	stand to support a book
devious	51	cunning
lithe	51	flexible; supple
wiry	51	thin
sinewy	51	strong; muscular
inadvertently	52	not on purpose; accidentally
vital	52	essential; critical
puzzlement	52	confusion; bewilderment
congregation	53	gathering; assembly
satanic	53	devilish; cruel
ecstasies	53	rapture
rabble	53	disorganized group; a mob
diabolical	53	satanic; evil
rancid	53	rotten; reeking

1-13

husband	54	carefully preserve and use
larders	54	storerooms; pantries
prolonged	54	extended; protracted
siege	54	assault; attack
reap	54	gather; harvest
nocked	55	placed a bowstring in a notched arrow shaft
longbows	55	bows held vertically (vs. crossbows)
marauding	55	raiding and plundering
parry	55	evade; defend against an attack; ward off a blow
debris	55	remains of something (often broken)
quarter staff	55	a long staff used as a weapon
cudgel	55	a short heavy club
retaliate	55	fight back; repay
oaken	56	made of oak wood
dappled	56	spotted; mottled
damson	56	small, tart plum
deduction	57	conclusion; inference
indignantly	57	with anger caused by something unimportant

uncanny	57	odd; mysterious
talons	57	claws
savage	57	fierce; untamed
savoring	58	enjoying; relishing
tranquility	58	calm; peacefulness; serenity
deception	58	trickery; artifice

1-14

damping	59	moistening
burgling	59	stealing; thieving
expendable	60	dispensable
basilisk	60	imaginary reptile with a look that kills
niches	60	crannies; openings
crevices	60	niches; gaps
spreadeagled	60	with limbs outstretched
ascent	60	climb
fissure	60	crack; crevice
rubble	61	broken pieces; debris
obsidian	61	a glassy black volcanic rock
sinuous	61	lithe; flexible
furtively	61	secretly; stealthily
lubricated	61	greased to work smoothly (and quietly)
inert	61	motionless; immobile
scrutinize	61	examine; inspect
tasseled	61	fringed; trimmed
dormitory	62	sleeping quarters
pistons	62	sliding valves in an engine
detachment	63	indifference; separateness
wraith	63	phantom
valiantly	63	bravely; gallantly
gouging	63	tearing out
onslaught	63	rush
appalling	64	horrifying; disgusting
bunglers	64	blunderers; ones who make big mistakes
exhilaration	64	excitement; elation
scuttled	64	scurried; scampered
laconically	65	briefly; tersely; concisely

1-15

prevailed	66	were continually present; predominated
subdued	66	quiet and unhappy; restrained
conciliatory	66	in a spirit of reconciliation/making peace
audible	67	loud enough to be heard
heartening	67	promising; encouraging
resolve	67	determination
uncharacteristic	67	not typical
gingerly	67	gently; delicately
tottered	68	stumbled
solicitously	69	in a concerned way
lush	70	profuse; rich

1-16

girding	70	fortifying; preparing
lych-gate	70	a roofed gate in a church yard
barbaric	70	savage; unrestrained
doddering	71	infirm; feeble
flailed	71	whipped; struck
barb	71	spike
piebald	71	of different colors
skulking	71	moving in a stealthy way; furtive
frenzied	71	excited to the loss of reason; wild

1-17

funk	73	gloom; depression
dispirited	73	without hope; disheartened
prestige	73	distinction; influence
stalk	73	track; pursue
ineptly	73	ineffectively; awkwardly
poleaxing	74	hitting as with a battle ax
pendantry	74	invented word: they look like jewels on a necklace
curtilage	74	ground within a fence surrounding a house
hummocks	74	mounds; piles
lanky	75	lean; gangly
ashen	75	pale
hefty	75	sturdy; strong
stag	75	male deer; buck
liberator	75	one who frees or releases
tipsy	75	drunk
outmoded	75	old-fashioned
lugged	76	heaved; dragged
haversack	76	bag like a backpack, worn over one shoulder
repast	76	meal; feast; banquet
clarification	76	explanation
tolling	76	ringing; chiming
top hole	77	excellent (slang)
ruminated	77	thought; pondered
nip	77	move quickly or briskly
tack	77	change directions
wheel	77	pivot
bob and weave	77	duck and spin to avoid injury
capital	77	first-rate; excellent
bung ho	77	go at it (without thinking of consequence)
yahoos	77	savages; brutes (*Gulliver's Travels* by Swift)
mess	77	mess-hall; cafeteria
curmudgeon	77	ill-tempered old man
diversion	78	distraction
loony	78	madman; nut
slack-jawed	78	with mouth open in amazement
pongo	78	smelly (slang)
impudent	78	audacious; impertinent
butterfingers	78	careless one
nimbly	79	quickly and alertly
sprawling	79	lying with limbs spread out
predicament	80	sticky situation; dilemma
elusive	80	evasive; slippery
serenaded	80	sang
ceaseless	80	unending; continual
cadences	80	recurring rhythm and pitch of a sound of nature
vigorously	80	energetically

1-18

archers	82	those who shoot bows
fletching	82	arranging feathers on an arrow
volley	82	simultaneous fall of numerous missiles
barrage	82	volley; shower
grappling hook	82	piece of iron with a hook or claw on the end to grab onto things
blunders	82	mistakes; errors
cascaded	83	fell steeply in a shower, like a waterfall
standard	84	banner; flag
undignified	84	humiliating

rent	84	tore
devastating	84	ruinous
devising	84	coming up with; inventing
lenient	84	mild
surly	84	hostile; sullen
petrified	84	horrified; frightened; frozen with fear
flaccid	85	limp; weak
sibilant	85	sounding like an *s* or *sh* does
tactics	85	strategy
spongy	86	not firm or solid
skirmish	86	minor fight
accursed	86	hateful
bloated	87	swollen; puffy
clapped	87	laid
jutting	87	protruding; sticking out
commando	88	military unit for raids into enemy territory

1-19

improvised	90	made out of what happens to be on hand
winded	90	out of breath; gasping
hammerlock	90	wrestling hold keeping the opponent's arm behind his/her back
uppity	91	insolent; presumptuous
posthaste	91	immediately; promptly
unencumbered	91	unhindered
doggedly	91	persistently; stubbornly
oblivious	92	unaware

1-20

jostling	93	shoving; pushing
whippy	93	springy
factor	93	consideration
plunder	94	loot; booty
initiative	94	independent action to support the group
spasmodic	94	irregular; erratic
sallies	94	ventures from a defensive position to attack the enemy
catapulted	95	sailed overhead as if shot from a catapult
varmints	95	animals considered to be pests; vermin
retaliatory	95	sent in revenge
rapidity	95	speed
javelins	95	spears
plummet	96	fall; plunge
ricocheted	96	bounced
demoralizing	96	disheartening
intact	96	whole; not damaged
bared	96	exposed; revealed
tinpot	96	small-time; unimportant

Chapter 11

Journal and Discussion Topics

1. How did the use of the moles to rescue Ambrose avoid a possible trap?
2. What details support the claim that the moles are careful tunnel technicians?
3. What do we find out is special about Martin's sword?
4. What important role does Cornflower play in this chapter?
5. What are the pros and cons of attempting a rescue of the Vole family? If you were Matthias, what would you do?

Summary

As Brother Alf is patrolling, he notices something moving on the ground near the Abbey wall. Matthias recognizes Ambrose Spike, and is about to rush down and bring him in, when Constance warns that it could be a trap. Matthias thinks about this for a moment and hurries off, returning with 6 moles who, after careful planning, tunnel out to Ambrose and bring him back. In the infirmary, the Abbot assures everyone that Ambrose is not in great danger, and soon, after a large dose of October nutbrown ale, Ambrose is able to tell his story. While warning the Vole family of the danger of Cluny's army, Ambrose alarmed Colin Vole who shrieked so loudly that he attracted a group of rats. They took the Vole family prisoners, attacked Ambrose with an iron churchyard railing, and left him for dead. He managed to crawl back to the Abbey. Matthias has an idea of rescuing the Vole family, but the Abbot and Constance read his heart and warn him that his idea is impracticable. Matthias realizes that without a magic sword like Martin had, he has little chance of effecting a rescue, and filled with shame and frustration, he weeps. Cornflower comes and comforts him, convincing him that he is growing more like Martin in both compassion and in the courage and leadership of a warrior. She ties her headband on his arm as colors for a warrior. She leaves, and Matthias speaks to Martin's image, thanking Martin for speaking to him through Cornflower.

Chapter 12

Journal and Discussion Topics

1. Do you think the setting is symbolic in this chapter? Why or why not?
2. What qualities and characteristics set Shadow apart from the rest of Cluny's horde?
3. For what purpose did you think Cluny wanted to send Shadow to Redwall, before he revealed his true purpose?
4. For what purpose does Cluny say he wants the tapestry? What other reason might he have?
5. Do you think Cluny is accurate in his prediction of what the loss of the section of tapestry will have on the inhabitants of Redwall?

Summary

Cluny calls for Shadow—a horde member who is rat, weasel, or a combination and who has special abilities. He describes in detail how Shadow can get into the Abbey in order to steal the section of the Redwall tapestry that depicts Martin the Warrior. Cluny predicts that because of the importance of Martin to the Redwall mice, the loss of his picture will be a devastating tragedy, leaving them leaderless and ineffective. He promises Shadow a great reward if he succeeds and dire punishment if he fails.

mossflower woods

quarry

the abbey

st. ninian's church

Chapter 13

Journal and Discussion Topics

1. How would you characterize the beliefs that shape the preparations made by Redwall inhabitants for the coming of Cluny?
2. How is the relationship between Cornflower and Matthias changing?
3. How do you think Methuselah knows what Matthias is thinking?
4. What do you make of Methuselah's story about Martin's sword?

Summary

The inhabitants of Redwall all prepare for Cluny's attack, either by gathering and preparing food, by learning the arts of self-defense, or by fortifying the Abbey. Matthias teaches quarter staff, while Constance gives instruction in cudgel and wrestling. After getting his lunch from Cornflower, Matthias learns in a conversation with Methuselah that no one knows where Martin is buried and that his magic sword may have been stolen by the sparrows who claim to have a treasure that belonged to the mice. Methuselah has not been able to pursue this information because the sparrows live high on the Abbey roof, and because he fears their erratic and violent behavior. Besides, he is not sure they are telling the truth about the treasure.

Chapter 14

Journal and Discussion Topics

1. The frog thinks that it is "none of his business" that the rats are creeping toward Redwall. What do you think?
2. Consonance is the use of multiple words that begin with (or, less often, contain) the same sound. When the narrator says on page 33, "the two old friends assessed the **B**eauteous **B**ounty of their lifelong a**B**ode," this is an example of consonance. Find an example of consonance in this chapter.
3. Compare and contrast Matthias's dream with Cluny's nightmare.
4. How do you think the mice will react to the theft of the tapestry?
5. What do you think will happen to Ragear?
6. Why does Cluny have Shadow steal the tapestry rather than open the gate and let the rat army in?

Summary

Cluny approaches Redwall with Ragear and Shadow. Silent and swift, Shadow climbs the Abbey wall. He follows his instructions, and proceeds to the Great Hall, where the door slams shut behind him. Using his fangs, he gnaws the picture of Martin free from the rest of the tapestry. In the meantime, Matthias is having a nightmare in which someone is calling to him for help. He wakes as he tumbles out of bed and realizes that the call comes from Martin and that aid is needed in the Great Hall. Shadow, hearing Matthias approach, bowls into him and runs off. The sentry mice join in the chase, and Constance comes running. Matthias catches Shadow's legs, knocking him down, but Shadow's vicious kicks to Matthias's head cause him to black out. Mr. Fieldmouse grabs Shadow at the top of the stairs, but Shadow stabs him twice with a dagger. Constance swings at Shadow to block a blow of the dagger, and Shadow falls over the edge of the parapet and lands in the road. Cluny, waiting below, runs up, grabs the tapestry, and abandons Shadow to his death. Ragear runs off by himself in the opposite direction from which the rats had come. The mice come out to try to catch Cluny, but they are too late. As Shadow says with his last breath, "Martin is with Cluny now."

STRATEGY 9

Characterization

Directions: Read the explanation, then answer the questions.

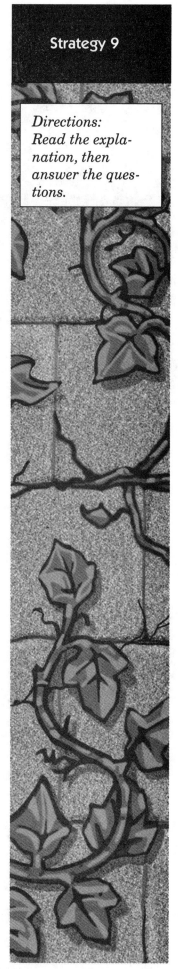

A **Character** in a story is someone or something whose actions, choices, thoughts, ideas, words, and influence are important in developing the plot. Characters are often people but also include other living creatures, and sometimes even non-living things. A force, such as good or evil, can operate as a character in a story.

Most stories have a single character or a small group of characters whose goal or problem is the core of the plot. This character or group of characters is called the **protagonist.** The protagonist does not have to be good, but a good protagonist may be referred to as the "hero" of the story. Readers usually identify with the protagonist and hope that the protagonist will succeed in attaining his or her goal. The character, group, or force that opposes the protagonist is called the **antagonist.** In certain stories, this character may be referred to as the villain.

Characters, whether human or not, have what we call "personality"—a set of characteristic traits and features by which we recognize them. Personality is what helps us distinguish one mouse from another mouse, one rat from another rat. **Characterization** is the name for the techniques a writer uses to reveal the personality of characters to the reader. Characterization is achieved in a number of different ways:

- **Words:** comments by the narrator, dialogue by others about the character, as well as the character's own words; what is said, as well as *how* it is said—dialect, slang, and tone—are important
- **Thoughts:** what's going on in the character's mind, the character's motives and choices
- **Appearance:** the character's physical characteristics and clothing
- **Actions:** what the character does
- **Interactions:** how the character relates to others
- **Names**: often symbolic of a major character trait or role
- **Chosen Setting:** the items, furnishings, etc., that the character chooses to surround him- or herself with
- **Change/Development:** the occurrence of and direction of change or development that a character undergoes inwardly

1. What techniques does Jacques use to characterize the moles?

2. What is the effect on you of the name "Cluny the Scourge"?

3. How does Constance interact with others?

4. What changes in Matthias's character have you seen so far in the story?

5. How would you characterize Methuselah and his role in the adventure so far?

Chapter 15

Journal and Discussion Topics

1. How does the setting of this chapter reflect the mood at the Abbey?
2. Methuselah says to Matthias, "I could see you were only putting on a brave face for the benefit of the others. That is good. It shows you are learning to be a wise leader. You hide your true feelings and encourage them not to give up hope." What do you think of this approach to leadership?
3. Methuselah's assessment of Matthias's approach is true in a way that Methuselah himself does not suspect. Explain how this is so.
4. How did his ease in descending the wall affect Matthias?

Summary

The Abbot addresses the inhabitants of Redwall, briefly rebuking them for unpreparedness, and then apologizing. He notes that the Abbey rose has withered and the tapestry is gone, and takes these as sure signs of sorrow to come. Matthias counters with good news (the recovery of Mr. Fieldmouse) and a speech of encouragement. While the others return to their duties, Matthias and Methuselah examine the damaged tapestry. Methuselah praises Matthias for hiding his true feelings in order to encourage the others, little knowing that Matthias is also hiding his true feelings from him. For Matthias plans to rescue the tapestry from Cluny, and is intent on deceiving Methuselah and Cornflower about the extent of his injuries in order to carry out his plot. Taking Shadow's dagger and a climbing rope, Matthias rappels down the wall of the Abbey and starts off toward St. Ninian's Church.

Chapter 16

Journal and Discussion Topics

1. What does Cluny want, beyond taking over the Abbey?
2. Philosophers differentiate between freedom—the exercise of the mind to think and choose as it pleases—and liberty—being able to physically go where one pleases and do what one wants. Why is this an important distinction here?

Summary

Cluny's army prepares for war, sharpening weapons and collecting ammunition. Cluny attaches the tapestry to his war standard, and sneers at the Vole family. Mr. and Mrs. Vole both defy him, but in vain. He has them locked in the hut behind the church until such time as he returns to kill them. Redtooth announces that the horde is ready, and Cluny joins them, as they give their war cheer and set out toward Redwall.

Chapter 17

Journal and Discussion Topics
1. Contrast Basil's attitude with that of the frog on the first page of Chapter 14.
2. What do you think will happen to Colin Vole in the course of the story?
3. Do you think Matthias was right to leave Redwall without telling anyone? Why or why not?
4. What do you think will happen to Matthias and the Vole family?

Summary
Ragear and Matthias both end up in Mossflower Wood. Ragear, hearing Matthias pass by, determines to take him prisoner in order to gain Cluny's favor. Matthias, noticing Ragear's approach, ambushes him and ties him up. As he considers how to cross the common land to reach the church, Matthias is startled by the appearance of Basil Stag Hare, a skilled military strategist who helps him cross the common ground. Basil then creates a diversion, drawing the rat sentries away and allowing Matthias to approach the church. Climbing in the window, Matthias begins to search for the tapestry, until he realizes that it is probably with Cluny on the road to Redwall. As he leaves, he hears pounding from the hut, where the Voles are beating on the door and calling him to get his attention. He rescues them and they begin to walk away when they are surprised by the returning rat sentries.

Chapter 18

Journal and Discussion Topics
1. Summarize the strategies used in the first skirmish (pages 82–84).
2. Asmodeus is evil, but not allied with Cluny. What role do you think a character like this could play in the outcome of the fight between good and evil as represented by Redwall and Cluny?
3. What do you think of Cluny's plan?
4. What is the difference between the way Cluny plans and the way the defenders must plan?

Summary
Cluny masses his army in the ditch across the road from Redwall. He plans to use grappling hooks and ladders to climb the wall, but the defenders knock over the ladders, and a beaver gnaws through the grappling hook rope. Many rats are injured. As the defenders cheer, Cluny has stones and arrows fired at them, and many are wounded. As Cluny plans a follow-up, the scene switches to Mossflower Wood, where Ragear is struggling to get free of the rope, when suddenly an enormous adder named Asmodeus approaches him and bites his neck, killing him. The scene shifts back to the ditch where Cluny is planning a surprise attack on the Abbey from within Mossflower, during which Redtooth, masquerading as Cluny, will distract the defenders before the Abbey's main gate. The attack group heads toward Mossflower, and Cluny sends off a party to hunt for a tree from which they can breach the Abbey walls. Two of the searchers, Cheesethief and Killconey, return in great distress. They have found Ragear's swollen and discolored body, as well as Asmodeus. Cluny warns them not to tell the others, and when the other search party returns, having found a suitable tree, they all go to the elm and make plans to climb it.

mossflower woods

Quarry

the abbey

st. ninian's church

Writer's Forum

Dialogue

Dialogue is a particularly powerful way to reveal a speaker's personality, thoughts, taste, and culture. The language that each speaker uses should reflect such important characteristics as age, education, and background. The level of formality the character uses should reflect the speaker's personality and approach to life as well as the social situation in which the speech takes place.

Dialogue can also reveal relationships. How 2 (or more) people speak to each other shows a lot about their feelings for each other. Do they give each other a turn to speak? What tones of voice do they use? Do they ask questions when they don't understand? Do they use polite phrases, slang phrases that they both know, more than 1 language?

In terms of text organization, dialogue can help to break up narrative passages, and can be more interesting than reported speech.

Punctuating dialogue shows which words are the exact words that the speaker said. Follow these rules:

- Put quotation marks around the words each speaker said.
- If the tag line that identifies the speaker comes before the quotation, put a comma after it, before the quotation marks.
- If the tag line follows the quotation, put a comma inside the final quotation mark if the quotation ends with a period. If the quotation ends with a question mark or exclamation mark, skip the comma.
- If you place the tag line in the middle of the quotation, place a comma before it inside the quotation marks and after it before the quotation marks.
- Start a new paragraph each time there is a new speaker, or if a speaker speaking for a long time switches topics.

1. Imagine that the rats succeed in climbing the tree and entering Redwall. Now imagine an encounter between a member of Cluny's army and a member of the Redwall community (not Silent Sam) as they meet for the first time. Write the dialogue that takes place.

Writer's Forum
Description

In a piece of descriptive writing, you let the readers know about the attributes of something so they can picture it in their mind's eye. You choose the features to mention based on what stands out among the physical properties and internal attributes of what you are describing, and these features will change depending on your topic. For example, if you were describing the setting of Redwall Abbey, you might choose features such as "layout," "function," "personnel," and "daily operations." If, however, you were describing a character, you would use different features: physical features, personality traits, actions, and habits. Here are some questions you can use to help you formulate your description:

- What is it?
- What are its attributes?
- How is it apprehended by the senses—look, smell, taste, feel, sound?
- How does it relate to other things in its environment or context?
- How can it be described by the 5 W's and How?

The way you organize the information you will use can vary depending on what you are describing. You can organize your description

- top to bottom
- front to back
- side to side
- inside and outside

- around the perimeter
- from the beginning to the end of its cycle or process

Source words that can help you express concepts of similarity and difference include the following:

- also
- and

- besides
- furthermore

- in addition
- too

1. Write a description of Basil. Then write a description of Cluny's dream (pages 28–29). Afterwards, write a brief reflection on the differences in content and organization between your 2 descriptions.

Chapter 19

Journal and Discussion Topics

1. Why doesn't Mr. Vole take the first opportunity to escape?
2. What occurrences lead Matthias to seriously mistake Basil's character?
3. What do you think might be the answers to Matthias's 4 questions on page 91?
4. What factors contribute to making Matthias falling asleep?

Summary

Matthias, the Vole family, and the sentries are all startled by their sudden meeting, and Colin and Mrs. Vole are caught. But Matthias and Mr. Vole stay free, and at Matthias's encouragement, Mr. Vole escapes into the woods. Matthias keeps the rats at bay while calling for Basil who pops up, having freed Colin and Mrs. Vole. At first, Matthias does not understand Basil's teasing because he thinks Basil abandoned him in the midst of the fight. They make peace as they trounce the rats, and plan that Basil will gather up the Vole family and take them home, while Matthias returns to Redwall. They also plan that Basil will return the Vole family to Redwall when it is safe to do so. On his return, though, Matthias, unsure of his directions stops to drink at a stream in Mossflower and take a brief rest. Here, he accidentally falls asleep.

Chapter 20

Journal and Discussion Topics

1. In what ways are Cluny's mental criticisms of his followers unjust?
2. As in this case where he tells exactly what Cornflower was serving for dinner, Jacques pays a great deal of attention to food. What do you think of this?
3. Which weapons are turning out to be the most successful?
4. What problems could the Redwall inhabitants run into if the siege continues?
5. How does Methuselah's discovery change the meaning of Cluny's theft of the tapestry portion?
6. What do you make of the phrase "three bags full"?

Summary

Cluny's attack party has made it into the elm, and although Cluny is generally disgusted with the group's performance (as usual), he has noticed a weasel named Scragg who shows promise. Cluny calls a halt to wait for evening, and Scragg shows initiative by suggesting a particular branch on which to cross to the Abbey wall. Cluny joins Scragg for a private conference in which he signals his approbation. Cheesethief, however, overhears, and begins to plot Scragg's overthrow. Back on the parapet by the front gate, the Abbot and Constance confer about Matthias's absence, and the Redwallers launch a new attack using a see-saw to send missiles into the ditch where Cluny's army still huddles. Now the rats begin to send up chunks of iron grave-railing, a deadly device, but one that often backfires, because if it doesn't reach the wall, it falls back upon the attackers. Meanwhile, Cluny awaits the time for his attack, and Methuselah contemplates the empty space in the tapestry and thinks about Matthias. As he puts his paw against the wall to steady himself, he discovers writing carved into the wall. He seems to think he has discovered a clue to the whereabouts of Martin's burial site.

Test 2, Book One, Chapters 11-20

Vocabulary

Look at each group of words. Tell why it is important in the story.

1. drag, traction, loam, topsoil

   _____

   _____

2. top hole, pongo, bob and weave, loony, curmudgeon

   _____

   _____

3. pulpit, choir loft, hassock, lady chapel

   _____

   _____

Essay Topics

1. What are the weaknesses in Cluny's organization? In Redwall's?

2. Write brief characterizations for 2 of the following characters: Cheesethief, Ragear, Colin Vole, the Abbot.

3. Think of another story in which a confrontation goes on for a good part of the book. How did the author keep your interest? How are Jacques's techniques similar and/or different?

4. What's your favorite moment in Chapters 11–20? Explain why.

5. How has Jacques changed the structure of the chapters from the way he organized them in the very beginning of the book. Explain why you think he did this.

6. Using at least 3 different kinds of animals as examples, explain how Jacques uses dialogue in creating characterization.

2-1

upbraiding	101	scolding; reprimanding
remotely	101	distantly; slightly
riven	101	split by a violent strike
confronted	102	faced; encountered
disarmingly	102	charmingly; attractively

2-2

prime	105	youth
unceremoniously	106	without ceremony
snaked	106	moved like a snake
venomous	106	poisonous
casualties	107	number injured; damage done
diversionary	107	distracting
coveted	108	desired exceedingly
riveted	108	rooted to the spot; paralyzed
fatalistically	108	without hope of changing the course of events
piteously	108	in a way calculated to arouse pity
bramble	108	thorn bush
masquerade	110	deception; pretense
reveled	110	rejoiced
plumage	110	finery; attire
consolidate	111	secure; make certain
resounding	111	unquestionable
tempering	111	moderating; blending
jubilatory	111	triumphant
maimed	111	crippled; mutilated
vanquishment	111	defeat
vanguard	111	troops leading an army
intertwining	111	linked; interlaced
heartily	112	energetically
eccentric	112	one who behaves oddly
credibility	112	believability
invincible	113	unable to be beaten
adjourn	113	end; close

2-3

racked	114	tortured; suffering
remorseless	114	unwilling to give up
vitality	114	life force; energy
flogged	114	whipped; beaten
concocting	114	making up; inventing
spectral	115	ghostly
impaled	115	killed by being run through
vixen	116	female fox; sly

2-4

quench	117	decrease; subdue
handiwork	117	work accomplished by hand
boisterously	117	in a noisy way
scallywag	118	rascal; scamp
mock	118	false; pretended
wry	119	ironic
spluttering	119	spitting
racking	119	stretching or straining
draught	120	drink; gulp
booby	120	dope; fool
affinity	122	resemblance; interconnection
retorted	122	replied; rebutted
scoundrel	122	rogue; rascal

fortifications	123	works erected to defend a place
chummy	123	friendly
adequately	123	sufficiently; well enough

2-5

salves	125	ointments; balms
potion	125	brew; elixir
induce	125	cause; bring on
enhance	125	improve; strengthen
oaf	126	dunce; fool
replenish	126	fill up
ingratiatingly	127	in a way intended to win favors
espionage	127	spying
gestured	128	motioned
modestly	128	in a way that preserves the established sense of what is proper

2-6

obliged	130	complied
amateurs	130	beginners; lacking in experience
impeccable	130	perfect; unable to be criticized
insatiable	130	unable to be satisfied
victuals	130	food; fare
tiffin	130	light midday meal (British)
tankard	130	tall mug, often with a lid, for beer or ale
suppressed	131	held back
musty	131	dank; stale
disintegrated	131	fell apart
ventured	131	proceeded
lintel	131	horizontal board that carries the load above a door
florin spikes	132	nail with a large rounded top the same size as an English florin coin
chagrin	132	annoyance
stature	132	status; prestige
depicting	133	picturing; portraying
valor	133	bravery; courage
effigy	133	likeness
burnished	133	polished
pristine	133	perfect
supple	133	pliant; flexible
tanner	133	one who treats leather
scabbard	133	cover or sheath for a sword
girdle	133	belt; sash

2-7

foxtrot	135	pun on the ballroom dance of that name and the word *trot*, which is slang for diarrhea
crestfallen	135	discouraged; disappointed
wheedling	136	coaxing; pleading
blandishment	136	flattery; adulation
cynical	136	distrustful
adamant	136	firm; unmoving
puny	136	feeble
milksop	136	unmanly male
noncommittally	136	ambiguously; without being definite
underhand	136	deceitful; sly
baffling	137	puzzling; mysterious
indulgently	137	kindly; tolerantly
reverie	137	contemplation
encased	137	enclosed

cunningly	137	cleverly
sheath	137	cover
rogue	137	scamp
leveret	138	hare under 1 year old
buccaneer	138	pirate; marauder
swashbuckler	138	daring soldier
fenced	138	fought with swords
cruets	138	narrowmouthed jars
filly	138	slang for lass; young woman
hinds	138	female red deer
lancejack	138	lance corporal (British slang)
ferment	138	agitated state
treatise	139	study; dissertation
concede	141	give in
admonitory	141	cautioning
surveillance	142	watch; observation
crick	142	cramp
dwindled	143	grew smaller; diminished in size
bestowed	143	conferred
apex	143	peak; highest point
precious little	143	not much at all
cursory	143	initial
piqued	144	provoked; angered
levity	144	lightness; humor

2-8

parchment	147	paper
servile	148	like a servant or slave
inwardly	148	to himself
pantomime	148	act; deception; performance
wager	148	bet
deploy	148	assemble; organize

2-9

quest	149	journey; mission
relics	150	remains; leavings
regally	150	majestically
ascended	151	climbed; mounted
abide	151	follow; stand by
Dame Fortune	151	Lady Luck; personification of luck
designated	151	appointed
infinity	151	forever; unlimited space
disconsolate	152	unable to be consoled
intricate	152	tricky; complicated
limbering	152	becoming more flexible or supple
sandstone	153	sedimentary rock used in architecture
alacrity	153	liveliness; quickness
projecting	153	sticking out
gargoyle	153	figure of a monster used as a rainspout or architectural decoration
plucky	153	courageous; spirited
gable	153	triangular roof part
treacherously	154	dangerously
agitatedly	154	nervously; uneasily
enlighten	154	inform
annals	154	historical records
dislodge	154	pry loose
descending	154	moving downward
resolutely	154	persistently; determinedly
notching	155	placing the bowstring into the notch on the shaft of the arrow

tenacious	155	persistent; obstinate
dispersed	156	scattered

2-10

deliberate	157	consider
rendezvous	158	meeting
nettles	158	stinging plants
midges	158	tiny flies
hacking	158	chopping
sniveling	158	whining; complaining
crony	158	associate; colleague
gizzard	158	innards; internal organs
pummeling	159	beating
hammer and tongs	159	with enormous force or violence
furrow	159	trench in the earth like that made by a plow
berated	159	scolded
renowned	159	well known; famous
slinking	160	sneaking
adversary	160	opponent; enemy
grit	160	dirt; sand
taut	161	tight
confiscating	161	taking away
gesticulating	162	gesturing

Book Two

Chapter 1

Journal and Discussion Topics

1. What, if anything, surprised you in this chapter?
2. What emotional states does Matthias go through in this chapter?
3. Do you think Matthias is to be blamed for his behavior? Why or why not?
4. What do you think the illustration conveys? (Use only with hardcover or Avon edition.)

Summary

Matthias awakes to the realization that his friends at Redwall Abbey are in danger. In humiliation he rushes off and blunders along until he is completely lost and is afraid of the sights and sounds of Mossflower at night. Hiding in a beech tree, he decides his behavior does not befit his role as a Redwall warrior, and hearing a noise at that moment, he steps out boldly and draws his dagger to defy the deadly danger. He is startled to find that a baby red squirrel (Silent Sam) has sneaked up behind him. Matthias is able to determine that the squirrel knows the way to Redwall Abbey and will lead him there.

Chapter 2

Journal and Discussion Topics

1. Why do you think Methuselah chooses to convey his message to the Abbot as he does?
2. Do you think the Abbot has good judgment? Why or why not?
3. Why does Cheesethief hate Scragg?
4. Do you think there will be any consequences to Cheesethief for his treatment of Scragg? Why or why not?
5. Jacques made the choice to have the murder of Scragg witnessed by Matthias and the baby squirrel. What do you think this contributes to the narrative?
6. The term "gentlemouse" on page 111 takes an English word "gentleman" and adapts it to animal life. "Henchrats" (instead of "henchmen") on page 21 is another example. Find 4 more examples in Chapter 1, Book One.
7. Compare and contrast how the Abbot leads with how Cluny leads.
8. Predict Cluny's future.

Summary

Methuselah points out to the Abbot that the tall elm is being used to breech the wall, and the Abbot sends Constance to address the situation. In the meantime, Cluny's raiding party up in the elm tree is trying to get a plank laid to allow them to cross into Redwall. Tension within the party grows when Cheesethief drops the end of the plank and Scragg, the weasel, guides the group to get it in place. As Cluny crosses the plank, Constance appears on the wall and kicks it, sending Cluny falling to earth, while Winifred the otter begins to use her sling. Cheesethief takes revenge on Scragg by shoving him out of the tree. The Redwall contingent recognizes Cluny, but they leave without checking to see if he is dead because they're concerned that the attack might be a diversion for a more serious attack elsewhere. Cheesethief discovers that Cluny is alive, and directs the res-

Book Two
Chapter 3, Page 114
Chapter 4, Page 117

mossflower woods
Quarry
the abbey
St. Ninian's church

cue operation to try to get in good with Cluny. Then he goes to check on Scragg, pretending that he's really concerned about Scragg's welfare. At the same time, the baby squirrel leads Matthias up to the Abbey Wall, just by the elm tree, so the 2 of them end up witnessing the return of Cheesethief and his murder of Scragg. Matthias and the squirrel enter the Abbey just in time to see the retreat of Cluny's horde. Some of the Redwall inhabitants want to wipe out Cluny's army, but the Abbot won't allow it. Cornflower and Matthias meet briefly, and she reports that her father is well. The Abbot elects Constance, Matthias, Winifred, Ambrose, and Foremole to take command of the Redwall forces, while he aids the injured and feeds the hungry. He sends Matthias to speak to Methuselah.

Chapter 3

Journal and Discussion Topics

1. Jacques uses the phrase "remorseless vitality" in describing Cluny on page 114. What do you think of this phrase?
2. Compare and contrast Cluny's second nightmare on page 115 with his first nightmare on pages 28–29.
3. Why do you think Cluny says, "Foxes?" after Killconey tells him about the vixen healer?
4. Look at the last two sentences of the chapter on page 116. Whose perspective is being expressed? How can you tell?

Summary

Cluny, suffering with his wounds, has another nightmare in which he fights the warrior mouse. As the sword is piercing his chest, he awakens to the sound of the Joseph Bell, and sends Fangburn, who had been trying to remove a piece of elm from Cluny's chest, off to find some new recruits. Fangburn returns quickly with a group of recruits. Cluny asks if any of them knows of a healer, and Killconey, a ferret, tells of a vixen named Sela who is skilled in healing. Cluny sends Killconey to get Sela, and at the same time sends Redtooth to find something that can be used as a battering ram.

Chapter 4

Journal and Discussion Topics

1. Why do you think Jacques placed the poem at the beginning of the book as well as here?
2. Describe Methuselah's method for solving the riddle.
3. What strategies do you use to figure out what Foremole and his fellows are saying?
4. What do you think they will find if they go down the stairs? Explain your reasoning.

Summary

Methuselah and Matthias finish applying ink to the lettering, and are able to read the poem. Taking the poem one sentence at a time, they solve the riddle: that Martin is still among them, living on in Matthias, whose name can be made by rearranging the letters of "I am that is"; that Matthias has a great task to perform and that he must find Martin's tomb and his sword. With the help of the moles, the flight of stairs leading to the tomb is discovered.

Writer's Forum   Summary

A **summary** is a useful tool for focusing attention on the major points made in a piece of writing that is too lengthy to remember in its entirety. A summary is a selection with a purpose: the same piece of writing could be summarized in more than one way, depending on why you want to recall parts of it. You choose what is most important to you at this time for this reason.

Here are some steps you can take:

- Identify your purpose for summarizing.
- Using your purpose as a focus, review the material, noting the main ideas in your own words.
- Write a separate sentence for each main idea.
- Organize your notes in a logical order for your purpose. (Often this may be chronological order or the order of appearance in the material from which you are summarizing, but other orders are possible.)
- As you write your summary, use transitions to show the relation of one idea to another.
- Review your summary to be sure it fulfills your purpose.

1. Summarize the events in Cluny's first attack on Redwall in order to identify the kinds of strategies each side uses.

Writer's Forum   Riddles

Riddles are metaphors that test our ability to perceive the world in a fresh and unexpected way. Riddles ask us to perceive likenesses, associations, and comparisons between items that may seem to us to have nothing to do with each other.

The word *riddle* means "to give advice," and riddles have often been used as an educational device. The oldest preserved riddles are school texts from Babylon. Riddles are also used to conceal information from all but those special few for whom it is meant. In *Redwall,* the riddle is written so that particular knowledge and insight not known to everyone are needed to solve it. This insures that precious information and a valuable treasure will not fall into the wrong hands.

To write riddles, think of an object and an unusual way to describe it. Or find another object that has something in common with it, but that people would not immediately associate with it.

When is a door not a door? When it is ajar. (a jar)

Using word play is allowed, too. You can insert a word with more than one meaning and hope the solver will mistake which one you mean.

How can you tell the chef is mean?
He beats the eggs and whips the cream.

1. Write 3 riddles. Trade with classmates and try to solve them.

Chapter 5

Journal and Discussion Topics
1. Who do you think is more clever, Cluny or Sela? Why?
2. How do you think the Abbot would respond to Sela's letter?
3. Do you think the rats will recognize Sela's treachery? What might give her away?

Summary
Sela, the vixen healer recommended by Killconey, takes care of Cluny. Her approach is a combination of herbal remedies and some hocus pocus, which Cluny easily sees through. Sela tries to leave Cluny's headquarters after she has given Cluny a sleeping potion, but the rats prevent her. She persuades them to let her speak to her son Chickenhound, and (on the pretext of giving him a list of herbs to obtain for her treatment of Cluny) slips him a note to the Abbot in which she offers to sell her knowledge of Cluny's plans for the next attack on Redwall.

Chapter 6

Journal and Discussion Topics
1. How did the illustration work for you in this chapter? How can you use what you learned for your subsequent reading? (Use only with hardcover or Avon edition.)
2. Frequently in stories of a hero, there is an adventure in which the hero must descend underground, undergo a testing, and return to the earth's surface somehow changed. How does this pattern apply to Matthias?
3. What is striking about the condition of the shield and sword belt?
4. What do you think the new riddle means?

Summary
Cornflower provides food for Basil and the Vole family who have all arrived safely at Redwall. In the meantime, Matthias and Methuselah descend the stairway that the moles uncovered and find a door. Matthias discovers how to open it by solving a riddle, and although the riddle states that Matthias is the only one who should enter the room, he invites Methuselah to accompany him. They find Martin's tomb, as well as a shield and a sword belt, and another riddle on the back of the door, underneath the place where the shield had hung. This riddle sets a task for Matthias to accomplish, using the shield at night under the moon.

mossflower woods

quarry

the abbey

st. ninian's church

Chapter 7

Journal and Discussion Topics

1. What do you think Constance has planned for the foxes?
2. What does "C'm'ere" mean (page 137)?
3. Methuselah and Matthias solved the first riddle themselves. Do you think they could have solved the riddle in this chapter without Constance?
4. If you were trying to help Matthias find the meaning in the events surrounding the solving of this riddle, what would you tell him?

Summary

Chickenhound comes to the Abbey with Sela's message, asking to see the Abbot. Constance convinces him that he has to deal with her, and sets up an appointment between the Abbot and Sela in Mossflower Woods, 2 nights hence. Constance thinks that Sela's "information" is part of a hoax, and it is clear that she, not the Abbot, will meet Sela in the woods and give her what for. Matthias goes to lunch with the Voles, the squirrels, and Basil, and Basil gives Silent Sam a dagger, making a sheath for it from a sandal. Methuselah calls Matthias from his lunch to reveal that he has discovered the threshold mentioned in the riddle: it is the gatehouse. They return to the riddle poem and decide that they must stand on the wall above the gatehouse at 1 in the morning, facing north. They go to the spot, and, after Foremole and his helpers move a pile of rubble for them, they discover a special circle cut in the stone. It is domed, with 2 slots and 13 circles, each with a smiling face. Constance comes by to remind them not to miss tea, and Matthias is sending her away when she notices what they are doing. She immediately identifies the 13 circles as the 13 full moons of the year, and points out to them that the shield would fit into the circle (the 2 slots fitting the handles), and would then reflect the moonlight, showing them by reflection the location of the sword of Martin.

Chapter 8

Journal and Discussion Topics

1. Explain how Cluny tricked Sela.
2. How do you understand Cluny's reference to chess?

Summary

Convinced that Sela is double-crossing him after hearing Fangburn's report of the message, Cluny plants a diagram of a second invasion of Redwall under his pillow with a corner sticking out. He stops taking the sleeping medication that Sela gives him, while pretending to her that he wants a stronger dose. He allows his 2 guards, Redtooth and Fangburn, to get drunk, and gives Sela permission to drink, but notices that she only pretends to drink. Cluny feigns sleep, and when he feels the pillow move, he knows Sela has taken the bait. Through an indirect report of Cluny's thoughts, the narrator reveals that the plan was for attacking Redwall with a battering ram, which is only a diversion: while the Redwallers worry about the ram, he will actually be attacking the Abbey from underground, tunneling under the southwestern corner of the Abbey wall.

Chapter 9

Journal and Discussion Topics

1. What do you think motivated the sparrows to attack Jess?
2. Characterize Warbeak.
3. Where do you think the sword is?

Summary

Martin, Methuselah, and Constance go to the ramparts to find Martin's sword. As the Joseph Bell tolls 1, Matthias lays the shield in the circle. They follow the path of the reflected light. . . to the Abbey weathervane, high atop the roof. Methuselah determines that the sword must be on the arm that points north. But the Abbey roof is enormously high. How can they reach the sword? Mrs. Squirrel (Jess) seems to be the obvious choice for the job. Everyone gathers to watch Jess ascend the roof. When she reaches the top, they see the weathervane move, and assume she is getting the sword. As she begins to come down, she is suddenly attacked by sparrows, and mouse archers shoot arrows to frighten off the birds. One sparrow is accidently wounded in the leg and falls to earth, just as Jess gets down. Constance removes the arrow from the sparrow's leg and traps the sparrow (Warbeak) under a rush basket. Jess reveals that although she saw the shape of the sword in the holder on the north pointer of the weathervane, the sword is no longer there. Matthias is wondering what to do, when the trapped sparrow begins berating him and threatening to kill him.

Chapter 10

Journal and Discussion Topics

1. Why do you think Sela shuddered when Cluny smiled?
2. A *traitor* is one who betrays a trust or who is false to his or her duty. Identify all the traitors in this chapter and tell who or what they betray.
3. Why do you think Sela and Fangburn return to Cluny rather than running away?

Summary

In order to get to Mossflower Woods for the meeting Constance promised, Sela tells Cluny that there is an herb she needs for his healing that can only be found in Mossflower Woods at night. Cluny pretends that he won't let her go, and then gives in, warning her that she will have two rat escorts but secretly believing that she can evade them and give the Abbot the false information that he has provided for her. When Redtooth and Fangburn (her guards) begin fighting with each other, Sela seizes the opportunity and escapes, making her way toward Redwall, looking for the Abbot. The rats go off in separate directions to look for Sela. In the meantime, Sela is grabbed from behind by Constance, who takes Sela's copy of the battle plan and knocks Sela senseless. Redtooth comes upon Sela and Constance, and Constance sees the opportunity for the one-on-one combat she had promised Redtooth earlier. He slashes at her with a cutlass, but she grabs the blade, knocks Redtooth over, grabs him by the tail, and swings him like a hammer-thrower would, tossing him away. He slams into a sycamore tree. Fangburn comes up and asks Sela where Redtooth is. Sela points out Redtooth by the sycamore, and Fangburn realizes that Redtooth is dead. Fangburn and Sela start off back to St. Ninian's, concocting on the way a story to tell Cluny.

Vocabulary

Look at each group of words. Tell why it is important in the story.

1. poultices, salves, potion

   _____

   _____

2. massive, sandstone, gargoyle, apex

   _____

   _____

   _____

3. buccaneer, swashbuckler, fenced, parrying

   _____

   _____

Essay Topics

1. What progress has each group—the Redwall inhabitants and Cluny's army—made toward achieving its aims in Chapters 1–10 of Book Two?

2. Think of a traitor in another story you know. How is this traitor similar to and/or different from the traitors in *Redwall*?

3. Do you think the Redwall inhabitants will be fooled by Cluny's trick? Why or why not?

4. If you were Jacques's editor, what is one thing you would suggest he change to improve the book?

5. How did you feel about Redtooth's death?

6. Imagine the scene when Constance shows the copy of Cluny's invasion plans to the Redwall inhabitants. Write the dialogue that occurs as they discuss their response. Make sure each animal's words are characteristic.

7. Sometimes in fantasy a forest or woods can be symbolic. Do you think Mossflower Woods is symbolic? If so, tell of what and explain why. If not, explain your reasoning.

2-11

conclusive	163 absolute; decisive
sustenance	163 provisions; food
repulse	163 turning back; overthrow
salvation	163 saving
mediator	164 intermediary; one who reconciles differences
infirmary	164 place set up for care and treatment of the sick
pensive	165 thoughtful
baggage	166 a contemptible young woman (slang)
erudite	166 knowledgeable; learned

2-12

beaker	167 glass; tumbler
impassive	167 emotionless
corroborate	167 confirm; establish
conspirators	169 traitors
hunter's moon	169 full moon following the harvest moon
deceptive	169 misleading; something that deceives
domain	169 territory
expenditure	169 using up
languorously	169 wearily

2-13

disgruntled	170 irritated; displeased
convict	170 prisoner found guilty of a crime
fastidious	171 detailed and exact
bats in the belfry	171 crazy; loony (slang)
liven	171 make lively
all bark and no bite	171 harmless (slang)
stir your stumps	172 move it; hurry up (slang)
sidled	172 crept
glutton	172 one who eats greedily
hussy	172 mischievous girl
shackle	172 something that restricts freedom by confining the leg or arm
bade	173 said
agile	173 nimble; quick; spry
joist	173 beam; timber
obscured	174 hidden
aperture	174 opening
lead	174 leash
extolled	175 praised
elite	176 the superior part
placate	176 appease; satisfy
demise	176 death; destruction
gabby	176 talkative
hastened	176 hurried
oppressive	176 burdensome; depressing
apprehensive	176 fearful; uneasy
scuffle	177 brawl
commotion	177 disturbance
condemnation	178 blame; accusation

2-14

arduous	179 strenuous; exhausting
hobble	179 something used to make it difficult for an animal to move; shackle
pinioning	179 restraining a bird from flight
peril	179 danger; hazard
propelled	179 forced; pushed
profusion	180 abundance
curlicues	180 a whimsical curved design
curvature	180 state of being curved
perilously	180 dangerously
inquisitive	180 curious; questioning
trenchlike	181 like a thin ditch made by a plow
defile	181 a narrow passage

2-15

prone	183 prostrate; flat
grisly	183 horrifying; disgusting
guile	184 deception; trickery
profusely	184 generously; many times
dispassionately	186 neutrally; without showing strong feeling
rasped	186 spoke with a grating sound
speculatively	186 thoughtfully
sheathed	187 covered; put away in a sheath
vigil	187 watch
reprovingly	187 in a scolding way; with disapproval

2-16

wrath	189 rage; fury
diverted	190 deflected
exhortations	190 urgings; advice
fledglings	190 baby birds
chaff	190 debris separated from seeds and blown away during threshing
cowered	190 crouched down in order to seek shelter from something or someone
edict	190 decree; order
rummaged	191 shuffled through
dubiously	191 doubtfully
trepidation	191 uneasiness
antagonize	191 make angry
indignity	191 humiliation
tyrant	191 dictator
warder	191 guard
eaves	192 lower border of a roof that overhangs the wall of the structure
deferentially	193 respectfully
fend	193 take care of
despot	193 tyrant
grandiose	193 characterized by being of less actual value than is thought or claimed
foolhardy	193 foolish
recrimination	193 accusation against one who has accused you
demote	193 lower in rank
mode	193 way
pretext	193 excuse
inflicted upon	193 caused to
illuminated	194 lighted
discriminate	194 distinguish
supplement	194 add to; enhance; augment
abhorred	194 detested; was disgusted by
vacantly	194 blankly; without emotion
conspiratorially	195 schemingly
irate	196 angry; furious
ditty	196 song; jingle

covetously	196	greedily
capered	196	danced
palliasse	196	thin mattress
deflected	200	diverted; sent something in a different direction
cheeky	200	bold; plucky
lunatic	201	crazy; very foolish
preened	201	arranged one's feathers
coaxing	201	wheedling; begging
dejected	201	gloomy; discouraged
pathos	201	behavior arousing pity or compassion
scoffed	202	jeered

2-17

conspiracy	203	plotting
cavernously	203	as wide as a cavern
cads	204	scoundrels
righteousness	204	sense of moral justification
dire	204	warning of an urgent situation
indignation	204	anger at injustice
woffler	204	one who blusters and talks rubbish as a delaying tactic (British slang)
curry favor	204	gain favor by playing up to someone
harangued	204	badgered
hapless	204	unlucky
lily-livered	205	cowardly
strenuous	205	difficult
basking	205	lounging
thwarted	205	beaten; stopped
blighters	206	people who are disliked or contemptible
enlisted	206	enrolled in the military
at ease	206	not in the respectful postion called "attention" (military term)
audacious	206	daring
censure	206	reproach
blackballed	207	voted out
apprehending	207	capturing
confrontation	207	meeting; dispute
pothole	207	sizable round hole in the ground
surging	208	rushing; moving quickly
gamely	208	resolutely; pluckily
pursuit	208	chase
decoy	208	lure; bait; fake
replica	208	copy; imitation
nincompoops	209	fools
lounged	209	loafed; relaxed
husk	209	shell; outer covering
vociferous	209	talkative
swindler	211	cheat; deceiver
foliage	211	leaves
scrumptious	211	delectable; tasty; delicious
lashings	211	an abundance (British)
voraciously	212	ravenously; with great hunger
brace	212	prepare; harden
venerable	212	time-honored; aged and distinguished

2-18

scudded	213	moved swiftly pushed by the wind
vagrant	213	wandering
pandemonium	216	chaos; disorder (from *Paradise Lost* by Milton)

sparsely	216	barely; scantily
latticework	217	crossed strips of wood or metal
prospect	217	expectation
void	217	empty space
blustery	217	blowing violently
giddily	217	dizzily
nerving	218	bracing; steeling
hurtled	218	fell swiftly; whizzed
inexorable	219	relentless; unstoppable
loomed	219	came into sight and reach
unhinged	219	unsettled
peeved	220	vexed; irritated
duped	220	fooled
mercilessly	221	without mercy

2-19

cutlery	223	silverware
blaggard	223	rude or unscrupulous (phonetic respelling of *blackguard*)
galvanized	224	roused
attuned	224	sensitive
retribution	225	payback
overlord	225	ruler
whim	225	fancy; notion
self-sacrifice	226	sacrificing one's own needs for the needs of others
wastebin	227	trash can
preparatory	227	as preparation
corpse	227	dead body
resuscitating	228	reviving; restoring breathing to

2-20

haze	230	light mist
scintillating	230	brilliant; sparkling
filigree	230	lacework
extravaganza	230	spectacular show
geared	230	dressed; outfitted
butt	231	large cask
cum	231	along with being
soothsayer	231	predictor of the future
rostrum	231	podium
miscreant	231	scoundrel
beseechingly	231	pleadingly
slain	231	killed
paraphernalia	232	apparatus; equipment
reverberated	232	vibrated

2-21

aura	233	sense
apparition	234	ghostly figure
wrench	234	pull; yank
relentlessly	234	without mercy
churlish	234	rude
begrudge	235	refuse
over the moon	235	delighted
bereft	235	deprived of; lacking
chappie	235	young fellow; lad
irrepressible	236	impossible to constrain
nosebag	236	meal (slang)
catering	236	kitchen; food preparation
gruel	236	porridge

scullery	236 pantry
fusiliers	236 soldiers armed with muskets
flagons	237 mugs; flasks; tankards
bally	238 euphemism for *bloody* (British)
quarry	238 pit where digging takes place
bounder	238 one with poor social behavior
shuttlecock	239 birdy used in badminton
buffer	239 affectionate term for older respected officer who would risk his life for his troops
tunic	239 uniform jacket
embellished	239 decorated
duffer	239 incompetent one
fagged out	239 slang for tired
play me up	239 bother me
stentoriously	239 thunderously; loudly
stealth	240 sneakiness; furtiveness
pillowslip	240 pillowcase
hefted	240 lifted with effort

2-22

untoward	241 unfavorable
trekked	241 walked; hiked
rapier	242 narrow two-edged sword
dissent	243 disagreement
ensued	243 followed; broke out
escort	244 accompany
sorrel	245 a plant

2-23

fusillade	247 volley; hail
sortie	247 attack; sudden rain started from a defensive position
morale	248 spirits
rappelled	248 descended by sliding down a rope
swagger-stick	248 cane carried by military officer
retaining	248 keeping; holding on to
befitting	248 suited to; due to
contingent	248 group
cumbersome	248 burdensome; awkward
sporadically	249 once in a while; infrequently
vestiges	249 remains
earthworks	250 battlefield fortifications made of earth

Chapter 11

Journal and Discussion Topics

1. The agreed on approach to the war for the Redwall inhabitants changes in this chapter: they agree that they have "a duty not only to defend but to retaliate" (page 163), and they intend "to win at all costs." What do you think of this change? Do you think it is consistent with the mission of Redwall as the Abbot has presented it? Why or why not?
2. How does Warbeak's use of language reveal her character?

Summary

Constance's report of the contents of Sela's message leads to a counsel at which the Abbot reconfirms his commitment to give his attention to healing and feeding and to rely on the commanders he has appointed to manage the battle. Matthias puts forth his belief that repulsing the enemy is not sufficient; they must retaliate. The implication is that if Cluny is not stopped once and for all, the war will continue forever (but this is not explicitly stated). The Abbot agrees and retires. The counsel makes plans and then they all go off to bed, except for Matthias who lingers to speak with Methuselah of his conviction that with the sword of Martin, they could win the war. The conversation turns to the captured sparrow, and Methuselah expresses his surprise that Matthias can understand her because the Sparra language is difficult to understand. Methuselah then recalls his conversation with a sparrowhawk whom he'd healed, who told him that the sparrows stole something of importance to the Abbey. They go to the sparrow's basket prison, and Methuselah threatens her with his dagger, inducing her to tell them that "King have a big sword!"—exactly what they wanted to know.

Chapter 12

Journal and Discussion Topics

1. What mistakes did Sela and Fangburn make that prove to Cluny that their story is made up?
2. What effect did Asmodeus's appearance have on you?
3. What do you think the last sentence, "The pathway to eternity was open" (page 169), means?

Summary

Fangburn and Sela tell Cluny their story: Redtooth left Sela and Fangburn to investigate a noise, despite their advice that he not go. When he did not answer their calls, they searched for him, but found nothing but marsh and bog. Fangburn's scratches came from walking into a big thorn tree. They contradict each other about the direction from which the noise came, and Fangburn's wounds are obviously not consistent with an encounter with a thorn tree. Fangburn almost agrees with Cluny's sarcastic suggestion that "three little pigs with wings flew down and gave you a toffee apple each," stopping only because Sela kicks his ankle to make him be quiet. In the meantime, Asmodeus discovers Redtooth's body and claims it for his own.

Chapter 13

Journal and Discussion Topics

1. What do you think of the way in which Matthias treats Warbeak?
2. How do you think the tension between the rats and the other animals in Cluny's horde will play out?
3. What details suggest that Killconey really does know about tunneling?
4. What do you think will happen to Sela and Chickenhound?

Summary

Matthias undertakes to tame Warbeak, leading her on a leash, hobbled with a brick. Whenever she behaves well, Matthias rewards her with candied chestnut. They happen by Methuselah's study, where the record keeper has discovered the Abbey blueprints, revealing a way to the roof from inside the building. This is important because the roof is the sparrows' territory and if their King has Martin's sword, it is probably there. In the meantime, Basil is superintending the effort to shore up the entrance where Cluny's diagram indicates that the battering ram will be used. Matthias sees Cornflower collect food for his mission to regain the sword, and pledges to take care of himself, not only for the Abby but for her. Matthias and Warbeak begin their ascent on the inside of the Abbey roof. Tension mounts between the two, and when Matthias trips, Warbeak jumps on him. Matthias pins her and threatens her with his dagger, but she is still defiant. So Matthias takes her to the ledge and pushes her off. Keeping her from falling to the floor by maintaining his grip on the rope around her neck, he demands that she promise to behave. Warbeak gives her word, and for the first time they call each other by name.

The scene switches to Cluny's camp where an argument is going on between the rats, on the one hand, and the weasels, stoats, and ferrets, on the other, about which species are superior and should be promoted to officer ranking in Cluny's horde. Cluny sends Sela and Chickenhound away and interviews Darkclaw and Killconey about tunnels, in which Killconey claims expertise. Despite Darkclaw's ignorance about tunnels, Cluny privately promises him a chance to rise, and then goes back to discuss tunneling with Killconey. They are interrupted by Cheesethief who has caught Sela and Chickenhound eavesdropping. Cluny orders them to be killed (but not explicitly: he says, "You know what to do.").

Chapter 14

Journal and Discussion Topics

1. What evidence supports the claim that Warbeak has experienced a real change?
2. What do you predict the sparrows will do with Matthias?

Summary

Matthias now trusts Warbeak enough to remove the brick hobble. The climbing becomes more difficult, and as they concentrate on Matthias sticking his dagger into the ceiling to steady himself, they do not notice a sparrow who spots them and flies away. As they inch ahead, the dagger comes loose, and Matthias is only saved from a deadly fall by Warbeak grabbing him and pulling him back from the edge.

mossflower woods

quarry

the abbey

st. ninian's church

Try as they might, they cannot reach the door to the sparrow's quarters. But then Warbeak suggests that Matthias cut her free: that will enable her to reach the door by flying. Warbeak opens the door, which swings down, creating a ladder that Matthias can climb. Matthias removes the leash and collar from Warbeak's neck and stows them in the haversack he has to carry food and gear, but Warbeak declares her intention to stay with him. They reach the next door, which opens inward... and walk into a sparrow ambush in which Matthias is immediately pinned to the ground and pronounced a prisoner by King Bull Sparra.

Chapter 15

Journal and Discussion Topics
1. How would you describe Chickenhound's attitude toward Sela now?
2. Do you agree that the Abbot was wise to "leave matters to Jess" (page 186)?
3. Is the Abbot's attitude toward Chickenhound consistent? Explain your reasoning.
4. What is Chickenhound's goal? What steps has he taken toward its fulfillment?

Summary
The rats attack Sela and Chickenhound and leave them for dead in a ditch, but Chickenhound is still alive. Disgusted with Sela's failure to outsmart Cluny, thinking very well of himself for having survived, and plotting further mischief, he drags himself toward Redwall Abbey and collapses by the ditch. Silent Sam spots him and Chickenhound is brought into the Abbey. At his request, he is taken to the Abbot. Chickenhound asks for water, but Jess tells him he must give them information first. The Abbot takes pity on him and says he can stay at Redwall, whether or not he gives them any information. Chickenhound thinks about this and then reveals that the battering ram is only a diversion so that Cluny can tunnel under the walls undetected. But when the Abbot asks him why he came, Chickenhound lies and says he wants justice done to the murderers of his mother, whereas in reality, he wants access to the wealth of Redwall.

Chapter 16

Journal and Discussion Topics
1. What does Matthias learn in his initial encounter with King Bull Sparra?
2. How are King Bull Sparra and Cluny similar?
3. How is Asmodeus like Cluny in terms of reputation?
4. Do you think Matthias will be able to escape from the sparrows? What strategies do you think he might use?

Summary
Matthias continues to lie pinned to the floor but spends the time looking around, and identifies, amid the untidy sparrow territory, the King's private chamber. At the same time, Warbeak is telling her mother Dunwing (the King's sister) the story of what happened since she was hit by the arrow. Suddenly King Bull Sparra demands to know why Matthias is there, and not believing his answer,

that he was helping Warbeak, he declares that Matthias should be killed. Only the intervention of Warbeak stops the sparrows from killing Matthias. They empty his haversack, and the King finds the candied chestnuts and claims them. He then puts the collar and lead on Matthias and gives him to Warbeak as a pet. Matthias begins to act silly, dancing and singing a foolish song, leading the king to conclude that he's crazy, which is just what Matthias wants. Matthias explains to Warbeak and Dunwing, however, that it's just an act. As they talk, Matthias finds out their family story. Dunwing's husband had saved the King's life and had died the previous spring in a battle. Bull Sparra had promised to care for Dunwing and Warbeak, but has forgotten his promise. His behavior is erratic and can be cruel.

Meanwhile, Matthias looks for the sword but can't find it. He is not sure whether Warbeak knows why he has come, and he is sure Dunwing does not know. He uses Dunwing's relationship to the king to find an opportunity to take candied chestnuts to the King, pretending to Dunwing that he only wants to win his freedom, while he actually wants to search the King's quarters for the sword. Dunwing and Matthias ask for Matthias's freedom, but the King demands more candy chestnuts, which Matthias cannot get. After they leave, Dunwing reveals that she has guessed that Matthias had another motive for visiting the king. She then tells Matthias how a king named Bloodfeather stole the sword from the Abbey, and how Asmodeus stole it from Bull Sparra. Dunwing's husband, Greytail, died trying to get the sword back at Bull Sparra's order. The story about Greytail's fight with the starlings was a lie concocted by Bull Sparra.

Matthias falls asleep wondering how he can possibly get the sword back from Asmodeus. He is awakened by two Sparra warriors who drag him off to see the king because Bull Sparra has recognized Matthias's belt as being of the same design as his sword case, clearly part of a set. When Matthias is brought into the King's presence, Bull Sparra demands to know where he got the belt, and Matthias begins his silly act, finally offering to give the King the belt. The King accepts the belt, and Matthias takes the opportunity to ask for his freedom, but the King wants to keep him in captivity so he can get more presents. Matthias is sure that if he hadn't given Bull Sparra the belt, Bull Sparra would have killed him, and he figures that since he planned to steal the scabbard back anyway, there won't be a problem with stealing the belt back, too.

Writer's Forum   Compare and Contrast

In a **compare and contrast essay**, you show the similarities and differences between 2 people, things, ideas, approaches, etc., and draw some conclusion based on this examination. You choose the categories to compare and contrast based on your purpose, and these categories will change depending on your topic. For example, if you were comparing and contrasting Asmodeus and Cluny, you might choose categories such as "role in story," "interactions with others," and "appearance." If, however, you were contrasting the setting in Chapter 1 with the setting in Chapter 2, you would use different categories. A Venn diagram shows visually what 2 or more subjects have in common and what characteristics they have that they do not share.

Here is an example:

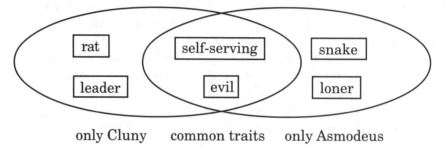

only Cluny   common traits   only Asmodeus

Source words that can help you express concepts of similarity and difference include the following:

- as well as
- similarly
- differ
- whereas
- however

- likewise
- alike
- while
- but
- on the contrary

- at the same time
- resemble
- conversely
- though
- on the other hand

1. Write an essay comparing and contrasting the role of food in Redwall Abbey and for Cluny's army.

Chapter 17

Journal and Discussion Topics

1. What are Jess's and Basil's motivations for recovering the tapestry?
2. The Redwall inhabitants changed their fundamental war philosophy in Chapter 11; here Cluny makes a vow that "never again would he allow himself to be thwarted by mice and woodland creatures." Is this a change for Cluny? Explain your reasoning.
3. Give evidence to support Jess's observation that the difference between the training of Cluny's horde and the Redwall inhabitants "was the contrast between slaving under a tyrant and voluntary cooperation that arose from determination and good fellowship" (page 206).
4. What might the restoration of the tapestry symbolize?
5. What was your favorite part of this chapter?

Summary

Jess and Basil conclude that it would be good for the inhabitants of Redwall, particularly the Abbot, to have the stolen tapestry returned, so they resolve to recover it. They sneak away from the Abbey without telling anyone. In the meantime, Cluny, having completely recovered from his wounds, is trying to get his horde back in shape by drilling them unmercifully. Irritable and irrational, Cluny has taken a vow that "never again would he allow himself to be thwarted by mice and woodland creatures." Basil and Jess happen upon them just as Cluny is striking a rat with his tail, and Basil interrupts to berate Cluny for his unseemly behavior. Cluny is enraged, and Basil continues, taunting Cluny, drawing him out onto the common, while Jess follows them secretly.

Wanting a one-to-one confrontation with Basil, Cluny commands his troops to stay well behind. Cluny jabs at Basil with his standard, to which the tapestry is attached, and suddenly backs Basil into a pothole, where the hare catches his foot and falls. Realizing that this is an opportunity, Basil calls to Jess, who comes dashing and snatches the tapestry, but then is reluctant to leave Basil with his wounded leg. Basil orders her off, but instead she grabs Cluny's tail, throws him off balance, pulls Basil's paw over her shoulder, and helps him toward the woods. But soon Cluny's horde comes after them, and Jess, exchanging the tapestry for a decoy made from a dishrag, sends Basil into hiding in the woods and lets the horde chase her into a horse chestnut tree.

Cluny orders the horde not to follow Jess up the tree. First Killconey tries to persuade her to join the horde, but Cluny shuts him up. Then Cluny threatens to kill her family, which at first enrages Jess, until she realizes what Cluny is up to. Then she pretends to be truly frightened for her family, and asks, sobbing, that Cluny promise not to hurt her husband and child. Cluny promises that if she drops the tapestry, he will (word of honor) not hurt her loved ones. Jess agrees, and drops the decoy. Killconey hands it to Cluny, who sees that it is a fake and screams with rage. Jess, safe in the tree, enjoys his reaction and speeds away through the foliage, arriving back at the Abbey in the early evening. She joins Basil, who has an exaggeratedly large bandage on his leg, at dinner. When Friar Hugo comes in, she solemnly pretends to have bad news, and tells him in stricken tones that Cluny has just torn up one of his dishrags.

Meanwhile, Methuselah begins the painstaking task of re-attaching Martin the Warrior to the Redwall tapestry.

Mossflower woods

Quarry

the Abbey

st. Ninian's Church

Chapter 18

Journal and Discussion Topics

1. What strategies form a part of Dunwing's plan?
2. What inherent dangers are there in the plan—how can it go wrong?
3. What do you think will happen to Matthias and King Bull Sparra?

Summary

One morning, Dunwing tells Matthias that he will be able to escape that day. Bull Sparra has blocked the door by which they entered the loft, so Matthias will have to descend the roof. Warbeak has gone to tell Methuselah to send Jess with a climbing rope to help Matthias down. In order to get the King and warriors away, Dunwing plans to start a false rumor: that Asmodeus is hurt in Mossflower and that he has the sword with him. As soon as the sparrows leave to recover the sword, Matthias must steal the belt and sword case and climb down.

Matthias is embarrassed because Dunwing knows that he did not come back to bring Warbeak to safety, but to get the sword. He apologizes, but Dunwing says she knew it the whole time, that the belt and the case belong to the mice, and that the sword and its accouterments have only brought trouble to the Sparra, including the death of her husband; for all these reasons, and also because he has been a friend to Warbeak, she will help Matthias. Warbeak returns. The message has been delivered to Methuselah, who has promised that Jess will be on the roof when the Joseph Bell rings for lunchtime. Matthias sees several potential problems with the plan. He decides he must trust his luck.

An hour before time for the Joseph Bell, Dunwing starts the rumor. Warbeak and Matthias are grieved that they may never see each other again, but their time for reflection is cut short by the King calling all the warriors. As soon as the warriors are gone, Dunwing calls Matthias and they rush to the King's chamber, and quickly discover . . . that the scabbard is gone from the back of the chair where the King had hidden it before. They search, and in despair Matthias knocks over the chair, revealing a hiding place beneath the seat where the scabbard and belt are hidden. They hurry out to the approach to the eaves.

Matthias, not being able to fly, has a difficult path to negotiate to reach the roof. He finds a rope, and Dunwing ties it around his waist and holds the end, flying out over the roof to support him while he climbs over the edge of the eaves. All goes well until the moment Matthias lets go of the rope with his hands to grab onto the edge of the gutter, and the edge breaks. Matthias falls, but Dunwing holds the rope tight and breaks his fall. But then, Matthias begins to slip. It is by jamming the rope into the broken edge of the gutter that Dunwing prevents Matthias from falling to his death. Flying under him, she then boosts him as he climbs back up, and he makes it onto the roof. Matthias climbs up to the weathervane, says farewell to Dunwing, and looks for Jess. When he spies her, he calls out, but she is slowed by the wind, which catches her bushy tail and pulls her back and forth. Meanwhile, King Bull Sparra, having found no snake and no sword in the woods, wings home just in time to hear Matthias call out "Look, I've got the scabbard!" He attacks Matthias, burying his beak in Matthias's shoulder. As a result, Matthias loses his balance and lets go of the weathervane to beat at the sparrow's head, finally knocking Bull Sparra senseless with the scabbard and causing them both to fall from the topmost point of the Abbey roof.

Chapter 19

Journal and Discussion Topics

1. Why do you think Chickenhound smashed or vandalized what he didn't want?
2. What strategies could Chickenhound have used that would have improved his chances of survival?
3. How did you feel about Cornflower's understanding of the meaning of Matthias's and Methuselah's lives and deaths on pages 226–227?
4. Were you surprised when Matthias was found alive? Explain your reaction.

Summary

While the Redwall inhabitants prepare for Cluny's invasion, Chickenhound has been left unguarded and is roaming the Abbey, stealing anything that strikes his fancy and destroying anything that doesn't interest him. He comes suddenly on Friar Hugo, who starts yelling for help. Chickenhound dashes away and comes upon Methuselah, who—having heard Hugo's shouts—had moved from the spot where he was repairing the tapestry in order to block the door. Chickenhound swings his sack of stolen goods at Methuselah and hits him in the head, unintentionally killing him.

Chickenhound escapes to the woods and runs, pausing only to listen for sounds of pursuit. Eventually he hears two pursuers: one a hedgehog and the other . . . Constance the badger. Fearing Constance, he seeks a place to hide, and finding a hole in the base of a dead oak, he throws in his bag and dives in after it. He listens, holding his breath, until all is silent again, and begins congratulating himself on his cleverness and anticipating his titles of renown. As he prepares to leave the safety of the tree, he reaches for his treasure sack and touches . . . Asmodeus.

At Redwall Abbey, everyone is mourning the deaths of Matthias and Methuselah, even though the search parties have been unable to find and recover Matthias's body. The Abbot tries to console Jess, saying that she is not to blame for Matthias's fall and that they will continue the search. The Abbot bemoans what he calls the "tragic waste of two lives." But Cornflower offers a different perspective: she says that both mice died in acts of bravery and self-sacrifice and that such lives are not a waste. Everyone present agrees.

Alf, heading out to lay the fishing nets for the night, invites Constance to come along and help. At the water's edge, he finds a dead sparrow and calls out to Constance. She pulls the corpse of King Bull Sparra out of the water, and sends Alf off for lanterns and help. In the meantime, she stomps through the water hunting for Matthias. Then the otters come and begin a calculated search. Soon a cry goes up, and Winifred swims across, dragging Matthias, who is quickly given into the Abbot's care. The Abbot resuscitates him, and as Constance carries him gently to the Abbey, the Joseph Bell tolls the message of the rescue.

mossflower woods

quarry

the abbey

st. ninian's church

Chapter 20

Journal and Discussion Topics

1. How do you think Cluny's treatment of the traitor rat affects his horde?
2. Why does Cluny want to make sure those at Redwall know he's coming?

Summary

The narrator points out Cluny's lack of appreciation for the beautiful morning as he prepares to lead his horde into the second attack on the Abbey. Having still not chosen a second-in-command, he keeps both Killconey (who has appointed himself drummer and calls the horde to order when Cluny wishes to speak) and his rat captains beside him. He has let it be known that he will make the promotion in the field. Cluny gives a speech to incite his army, and one of the rats calls Cluny's bravery into question. Cluny leaps upon him and kills him to set an example to the rest. They plan to march boldly up to the gates and attack early the next day.

Chapter 21

Journal and Discussion Topics

1. What do you think Matthias's dream means?
2. How do you feel about Basil's response to Matthias's desire to be left alone?
3. How seriously hurt do you think Basil is? Why?
4. Matthias has already left the Abbey secretly once, and felt guilty for not having told his fellows where he was going. Do you think he is justified in doing it again? Why or why not?

Summary

Matthias has a dream in which he sees Methuselah, who bids him farewell; meets Martin and Asmodeus; and is stopped by Martin from getting the sword because Martin wants to warn him about Asmodeus. His dream fades into reality as Martin's words "Hold him still now," turn out to be the Abbot's words, as he asks Brother Alf to keep a tight hold on Matthias so he can pull the piece of Sparra beak out of Matthias's shoulder. Matthias comes to and discovers the Abbot healing him, Alf holding him, Cornflower standing nearby, and Basil in the next bed, supposedly recuperating from the leg injury he incurred while retrieving the tapestry. Matthias exclaims about the joy the recovery of the tapestry will give Methuselah, and the Abbot takes this opportunity to clear the room and tell Matthias about Methuselah's death. Matthias is devastated and withdraws into himself for days, until Basil suggests to him that Methuselah would want him to get out of bed and live again. Basil and Matthias enjoy lunch together, and Matthias pumps Basil for information about Asmodeus, overcoming Basil's initial reservations about discussing the adder. After offering help, and making it clear that he really doesn't know much, Basil suggests that Matthias seek out an owl called Captain Snow, while warning that Captain Snow is extremely dangerous. Basil gives Matthias a medal that Captain Snow gave Basil for saving Captain Snow's life, claiming that if Captain Snow sees the medal before he sees Matthias, he won't eat him and may be able to help him with information about Asmodeus. Basil and Matthias both nap, but Matthias awakens first. He packs food, collects his dagger and a stout pole, sneaks out of the Abbey into Mossflower, and heads toward the deserted farmhouse near which Captain Snow lives.

Chapter 22

Journal and Discussion Topics

1. How does Matthias's manner change once he holds the stone? How do you account for this?
2. How would you characterize the shrews?
3. Reread the final line of Chapter 22. What do you think happens to Matthias?

Summary

Heading toward the farmhouse, Matthias finds his way blocked by a mouselike creature who accuses him of trespassing on shrew property. The challenger turns out to be Guosim, a member of the Guerrilla Union of Shrews in Mossflower. When Matthias defies her, he suddenly finds himself surrounded by 50 shrews. Log-a-Log, an older shrew, comes forward with a speaking pebble, which gives some order to the conversation. Matthias becomes placating and explains his relationship to the Abbey. Log-a-Log calls for a vote, and breaks a tie, voting that Matthias be allowed to go free. But Guosim snatches the pebble and demands that Matthias reveal his destination. Matthias explains the plight at Redwall and his need to find Captain Snow. But as soon as Captain Snow's name is mentioned, all the shrews flee into hiding. After a minute, Guosim and Log-a-Log return and try to dissuade Matthias from his mission. Matthias just asks them to point him in the right direction; Log-a-Log insists that the shrews escort him. Just before dawn, they approach the farmhouse. The shrews retreat, and Matthias tiptoes into the barn. Hoping to see the owl, he climbs some packed straw, but he slips and falls down the straw into the mouth of a ginger cat!

Chapter 23

Journal and Discussion Topics

1. What was the effect on you of getting no further information about Matthias's fate in this chapter?
2. What would you do about the battering ram if you were the mice?
3. Make a suggestion about what Jess could do with the barrel that would be, in your opinion, most effective.

Summary

On the parapet, Basil, the Abbot, and Constance discuss Matthias's absence. Suddenly Constance points out the approach of Cluny's army, confirming the fox's warning. Cluny arrives and demands surrender, but Constance defies him. Cluny signals an attack, but due to a tactical error, the sun is in their eyes, and the attack is ineffective. Cluny has to call a withdrawal almost as soon as the battle is joined, having already lost 4 rats and Killconey's drum, which Jess rappels down to collect. After midday, a crew of rats attacks the Abbey door with the battering ram; and Cluny sends Killconey to collect the tunneling party that will start work after dark. Although the defenders are sure that the tunneling will take several days to accomplish, the moles begin their monitoring. Meanwhile, the Redwallers worry about the damage to the Abbey door. Jess explains to Sam that she wants to put something in the drum and drop it on the horde, but isn't sure what to use. Later in the enemy camp, Scumnose brings Killconey the message from Cluny to start the tunneling.

STRATEGY 10 Imaging

*Directions:
Read the expla-
nation, then
answer the ques-
tions.*

The meaning of a work of literature is not captured first and foremost in words we use to speak or write about it. It is felt in our experience as we read and enter into the story. In the act of reading, the words of a book are translated into experience by the reader, an experience that for many readers can (and should if possible) include images and feelings.

Writing instructor Janet Burroway explains that "Fiction tries to reproduce the emotional impact of experience. And this is a more difficult task, because written words are symbols representing sounds, and the sounds themselves are symbols representing things, actions, qualities, spatial relationships, and so on. Written words are thus at two removes from experience. Unlike the images of film and drama, which directly strike the eye and ear, they are transmitted first to the mind, where they must be translated into images [by the reader]."

Different texts foster different amounts and different kinds of imagery and feeling (also called "affect"). This can result from the author's use of more or less description, the author's focus on abstractions as opposed to concrete things, a very complex writing style, or academic diction, etc. So your **imaging** won't always be exactly the same. Even when your imaging is at its most vivid, it is likely that it will not be as specific as a photograph or movie is, for example. The visual images we create in our minds are characteristically not sharp and finely focused, a quality that literary critic Wolfgang Iser calls "optical poverty." This is an important point, because you shouldn't expect these images to be something they're not, or force them into a mold. Just let them come into your head, watch them, and take note.

1. In order to keep track of your imaging, it is useful to write about or draw what you've seen. You might want to record the most striking image(s) that you recollect from each chapter. Don't worry about your drawing ability; just do the best you can in whatever medium is most comfortable for you or conveys best what you want to communicate about your experience.

Test 4, Book Two, Chapters 11–23

Vocabulary

Look at each expression. Tell what it means. Then tell who says it and why.

1. "bats in the belfry" (page 171)

   _____

2. "all bark and no bite" (page 171)

   _____

3. "stir your stumps" (page 172)

   _____

4. "There was no fool like an old fool." (page 188)

   _____

5. "as thick as thieves" (page 203)

   _____

6. "Friends in need are friends indeed." (page 219)

   _____

7. "It was touch and go." (page 234)

   _____

8. "took the wind out of their sails" (page 247)

   _____

Essay Topics

1. Compare the progress of Cluny's second attack to the achievements of his first.

2. Do you think Redwall is in more danger now from the battering ram or the tunneling? Where would you concentrate your efforts if you were leading the Redwall party? What might you do that would be proactive, not just reactive?

3. Do you think Matthias will succeed in regaining Martin's sword? What price do you think will have to be paid? How do you think the sword will figure in the outcome of the story?

4. Why do you think Jacques named the section you just finished "The Quest"?

5. How did you feel about Sela's and Chickenhound's deaths?

6. If you were Constance, how would you feel right now about Matthias's absence? What would you do?

7. What role do you think the shrews will have in the rest of the story?

3-1

sniping	255	shooting at exposed enemy soldiers from a concealed place
scathingly	255	painfully
shirking	255	lazy; loafing
dudgeon	256	indignation
sheepishly	256	in an embarrassed way
monotonous	257	repetitious
gravity	257	seriousness
milled	257	moved within a confined area but without purposeful direction
myriads	257	a seemingly endless amount
saturating	257	soaking
antics	258	funny or playful actions
obsession	259	overwhelming preoccupation
bolt	259	metal rod
brusquely	260	impatiently
contraption	260	device; apparatus
zenith	260	peak
incompetents	260	inept and inadequate creatures
entitlement	261	privilege
languidly	261	lazily
exalted	261	high-ranking

3-2

indolent	262	lazy
hereditary	263	passed from one generation to the next
ramshackle	263	broken down; ready to collapse
platitudes	263	clichés
atrocious	263	hideous
regurgitating	263	vomiting
rescinded	264	revoked; took back
rift	264	break; split
fatalism	264	hopelessness
desist	264	cease
meditations	264	thoughts; reflections
convey	264	give; deliver
bars	265	stripes
colossal	265	huge
orbs	265	spheres
bilked	265	cheated
huffily	266	testily
macabre	266	gruesome
raucously	266	harshly; noisily
chortled	267	chuckled
illustrious	268	distinguished; celebrated
cleave	268	stick; adhere
taunts	268	insults
jibes	268	teasing
expectant	268	anticipatory; waiting
contempt	268	scorn
militant	270	aggressive; ready for combat
mêlée	270	brawl; free for all
fray	270	disorderly fight

3-3

scoured	271	thoroughly explored
discern	271	make out; see
jovial	273	good-humored
stolen a march	274	gained advantage while unobserved
afoot	275	in the works; in progress

3-4

frugal	277	thrifty
disputes	278	arguments
breeching	278	breaking through(misspelling: should be breaching)
spanning	278	constructing a bridge over
fallow	278	unplanted; unproductive
puddenheaded	279	foolish (for puddingheaded)
surlily	279	irratably; sullenly
disembarked	279	landed; left the boat
elapse	280	pass by
disc	280	circle (disk)
coherent	281	sensible; able to speak
slithering	281	the sliding movement of a snake
tortuously	281	with repeated winding
defunct	281	broken; not working
scant	281	scarce
stark	281	grim; desolate
spectrum	282	range of color
umber	282	a dark yellowish brown
Indian file	282	single-file
stunted	282	undersized

3-5

fruition	284	fulfillment; realization
leverage	284	the action of a lever
block and tackle	284	pulley blocks used for lifting
ingenuity	285	genius; cleverness
sacking	285	bags
filter	285	go one by one
unabated	285	without stopping
decimated	286	massacred
even keel	286	balanced; level; steady
tamped	286	packed down
countrified	287	rural
dialect	287	language variation particular to a region
drenching	288	soaking
inferno	288	blaze; conflagration
holocaust	288	destruction; annihilation

3-6

slab	290	thick block of rock
reptilian	290	related to reptiles; cold-blooded and villainous

sinister	291	ominous; foreboding
anteroom	291	outer room
repulsive	291	revolting; sickening
phosphorescent	291	gleaming in the dark
recesses	291	alcoves; crannies
subterranean	291	underground
quell	292	subdue; overcome
recoiled	292	drew back
vile	292	evil; repulsive
pommel-stone	293	knob on the hilt of a sword
exhalations	293	outward breaths
opaque	293	not transparent
throes	294	torments; agonies
amplification	294	an increase
intruders	294	trespassers; prowlers
girth	294	circumference; perimeter

3-7

straight as a die	295	honest and trustworthy (British slang)
stave off	295	hold off
cauldrons	297	pots
tipstaves	297	staffs with metal tips
ritual	297	ceremony
malcontents	297	those who are unsatisfied; dissenters
avenger	298	one who pays back
nemesis	298	one who brings vengeance or justice to an evil-doer
ominously	298	in a way that foreshadows evil
deluge	298	downpour
headstone	299	grave marker

3-8

cul-de-sac	302	dead end
trance	302	stupor
dilate	303	enlarge
dominated	303	bent him to their will
undertone	303	murmur
lethargy	303	fatigue; exhaustion
exertion	304	effort; struggle
flecked	304	spotted; speckled
severed	304	cut off

Book Three

Chapter 1

Journal and Discussion Topics

1. If you were Cluny, how would you try to recover the battering ram situation?
2. What do you think of Constance's conclusion that to dismantle the horde, all that is necessary is to get rid of Cluny?
3. What similarities do you find between Cheesethief and Chickenhound?
4. How do you think Constance will discover that she has not killed Cluny? How do you think she will react?

Summary

The invasion continues through the night. Cluny is displeased with the slow progress of the tunnel, but content with the continued efforts with the battering ram. Having gained a new respect for Cheesethief (who had put himself in charge of that operation), Cluny has mentally promoted him to second-in-command. In the meantime, the Redwall commanders are assessing the situation, and Basil's opinion is that in half a day, the battering ram will break through. Jess arrives on the scene with the barrel, loaded with a hornets' nest that she intends to drop on the battering ram crew. This will be followed by 2 buckets of vegetable oil to make the ram impossible to handle. These steps taken, they retire to avoid the hornets. Cluny's troops also retire into the tunnel—as many as will fit there—while others of the horde have dived into a small pond across the meadow.

As a result of the hornet attack, there are 10 dead and many injured. Cheesethief comes to report the impossibility of continuing with the battering ram—it is too slippery to hold. Cluny sends Cheesethief to regroup the army across the meadow. At the Abbey, they check the damage to the door, and Constance comes up with a new plan. She believes that if Cluny were gone, the horde would disband. She notices that she can see shadows in Cluny's private tent, and imagines that with a powerful bow, she could shoot him and end the war. Working with a beaver, she makes the bow, sets it up, and waits for mid-afternoon for the best shot. However, unknown to Constance, Cluny has come up with another plan for attacking the Abbey, and taking 30 rats to help him, he goes into Mossflower Woods, leaving Cheesethief in charge of operations in the field. Being ambitious, Cheesethief interprets this move as the promotion he's been waiting for. He enters Cluny's tent, finishes Cluny's lunch, and dons Cluny's armor. The Joseph Bell tolls—the signal that Constance has been waiting for. She thinks she sees Cluny in full battle regalia, and shoots her arrow. The bow works perfectly.

The labels in the image read: Mossflower Woods, Quarry, the Abbey, St. Ninian's Church

Chapter 2

Journal and Discussion Topics

1. What aspects of Squire Julian's character are surprising in a cat?
2. When Squire Julian says "one," what does he mean (page 263)?
3. What does Captain Snow mean by "deader than an icicle in hell" (page 268)?
4. Matthias says, "I always remember who my friends are, and I never forget an injury done to me!" Do you think this is a good philosophy to live by? Why or why not?

Summary

The cat spits Matthias out of his mouth and stares at him in disgust, finally poking him with a paw and telling him to get up. Matthias stands up, shaking, and the cat demands an apology. Matthias apologizes and introduces himself, and the cat says his name is Squire Julian Gingivere, but he's willing to be known as Julian. He asks Matthias to clean himself up and explain his presence in the barn. As Matthias tells of his quest, he discovers that Julian knows Captain Snow; in fact, they had been good friends but have had a falling out and are not speaking to each other. As Julian gives Matthias a ride on his back to take him to Captain Snow's hollow tree, he gives Matthias a message for the shrews, whom he spots, although they are trying to hide from him. The message is that they may come to the barn and take what they will, but they must not argue and fight so much. Julian is a vegetarian, except for an occasional fish, and is not a danger to them.

Julian brings Matthias near Captain Snow's tree and then leaves. He asks Matthias to tell Captain Snow that they can only resume their friendship if Captain Snow apologizes. Then he warns Matthias to be careful and leaves. Suddenly, the owl swoops down, knocking Matthias flat on his back and seizing the medal. Matthias tells him that Basil gave him the medal and repeats the message from Julian. Matthias refuses an invitation to join Captain Snow in his nest, and asks him about Asmodeus. Captain Snow warns Matthias about Asmodeus and sneers that Matthias can never recapture the sword. Matthias is moved to anger and speaks defiantly, only arousing Captain Snow's laughter. Matthias bets Basil's medal that he, Matthias, can fight Asmodeus and win. The Captain agrees to the bet. If Matthias recovers the sword, Captain Snow will return the medal and promise never to eat another mouse or shrew. In addition, Captain Snow will apologize to Julian on bended knees. Captain Snow then tells Matthias that Asmodeus can be found in the quarry, and taunts him as he leaves.

Matthias returns to Mossflower where the shrews greet him and quickly begin quarreling and fighting among themselves. Matthias grabs the pebble and bitterly chastises them for having let him go into the barn without warning him about Julian. Log-a-Log takes up the stone and apologizes. He says that it was an oversight caused by their shrewish nature, which leads them to bicker and quarrel over little things and forget the important issues. Matthias says he will forgive them this once, but he also explains that his approach to life is to remember who are his friends and never forget an injury. He then explains to them the promise Captain Snow has made: that if Matthias defeats Asmodeus, Captain Snow will never eat a shrew again; he adds that Julian has given the shrews free access to the barn. He waits for the impact of this to sink in, hoping that they will be grateful and therefore willing to lead him to the quarry. But a shrew picks up the stone and tells Matthias that the quarry is not in shrew territory so they cannot. Log-a-Log is so angry he strikes the speaker. Guosim takes the stone and reprimands Log-a-Log, and a riot breaks out. Finally, Matthias grabs the

mossflower
woods

quarry

the abbey

st. ninian's
church

shrew and threatens him if he doesn't reveal the direction of the river to the quarry. The shrew points northeast, and Matthias, holding the stone, tells the shrew he doesn't need him, throws the stone away into the woods, and sets out alone.

Chapter 3

Journal and Discussion Topics
1. How does Cluny turn the death of Cheesethief to his advantage?
2. What do you think is Cluny's "second scheme"—the one being worked on in Mossflower?
3. What does Jess mean by "a warm reception for those filthy vermin " (page 275)?

Summary
Constance realizes that she has killed the wrong rat. At the same time, Cluny is realizing that something is wrong in the camp. He quickly comprehends that the arrow that killed Cheesethief came from the Abbey and was meant for him. Cluny turns the situation to his advantage by pretending that the death of Cheesethief by an arrow from the Abbey was part of a plan he had hatched. This is the scenario Cluny presents to the horde: recognizing that Cheesethief was ambitious and abusing other members of the horde, Cluny used his knowledge that Constance was planning to kill him to make sure that Cheesethief would be in his place when the blow fell, getting rid of Cheesethief and fooling the Redwall inhabitants at the same time. After this, Scumnose reports having found a family of dormice. Cluny identifies the leader and puts them under guard. He then reflects that although some things have gone wrong for him, he now has 3 approaches to taking over Redwall, one of which involves the dormice in a method that the narrator does not elaborate. Back at the Abbey, Jess is suspicious because the behavior of the horde has changed, and Cluny has been less in evidence. The Redwall inhabitants discuss this and wonder together where Matthias is. Jess says that they must protect Redwall so that Matthias has a home to return to, and they return to the battle.

Chapter 4

Journal and Discussion Topics
1. Log-a-Log is concerned with the shrews' democratic principles. Matthias cuts off his explanation saying, "You are either with me or against me." Is it the process or the product that is important, or is there an alternative way of looking at this issue? Explain your views.
2. In your own words, explain the strategy the shrews and Matthias used for spotting Asmodeus. Do you think there is anything they could have done differently that might have prevented Mingo's death?
3. What do you think will happen to Guosim?

Summary
Matthias goes to sleep, thinking of the shrews' betrayal. He awakes before dawn, knowing that the shrews have joined him, but he does not acknowledge

their presence. After Matthias eats, Log-a-Log apologizes and explains that the majority of shrews voted to accompany Matthias. Matthias ignores him, and Log-a-Log explains the importance of democratic principles to the shrews. Matthias says bluntly that he doesn't care about their process: they are either for him or against him. Log-a-Log announces that they are for him. They break camp and head toward the quarry. After lunch by the river, Log-a-Log takes the shrews across the river on a tree trunk. Matthias and Log-a-Log conceal the ferry and plan an ambush, not to trap Asmodeus, but to spot him so they can find the entrance to his lair. They spread out and watch for the adder. After a long wait, a shrew comes to Matthias and sends him to Guosim. On the way, Matthias meets Log-a-Log who tells him that Guosim is in shock. They get her into the water, and she finally tells them that Asmodeus has been there and killed a shrew named Mingo. They set off to follow his slithering tracks and reach the quarry. Log-a-Log orders all the shrews to retire, and only he and Guosim stay with Matthias. They sleep and then at dawn begin the descent into the quarry, fairly sure that Asmodeus will not hunt this day since he has just eaten. They pause for lunch at noon, believing that they have only half a day left in which to find the snake. As they stand up to continue the search, Guosim leans against a narrow slab and falls through, revealing to the others the entrance to Asmodeus's lair.

Chapter 5

Journal and Discussion Topics

1. Why would Cluny, who doesn't follow any rules, not use fire?
2. Do you think Cluny's mind has snapped? Why or why not?
3. What might have happened if Cornflower was not serving soup when Cluny and his horde put up the siege tower?

Summary

It turns out that Cluny's third scheme is a siege tower, and Killconey supervises its construction. Cluny plans that when darkness falls, Fangburn will intensify the attack on the gatehouse as a diversion, while Cluny leads the attack with the siege tower. Cluny signals Fangburn to begin the attack, and Constance, sensing a change, rallies the Redwall inhabitants, while Basil directs the bowmice and Winifred leads the slingers. Cluny and Killconey bring up the siege tower, and at the same time, Cornflower, who has been left in charge of the kitchen, leads the servers to bring food to the fighters, lighting the way with a lantern. Suddenly over Brother Rufus's shoulder, Cornflower sees the siege tower with Cluny on top. She shrieks and throws the lantern, accidentally setting fire to the tower and starting a rampage among the rats. Cluny tries to keep the rats on the tower until Darkclaw and Fangburn pull him away, just before the tower collapses. They wonder if Cluny's mind has snapped. Constance and the Abbot survey the damage, and give thanks that the woods did not catch fire. As morning comes, Cornflower amuses herself with the thought that a few hours before she was a heroine, and now she is back to being a cook. She wonders what Matthias would think if he knew.

mossflower woods

quarry

the abbey

st. ninian's church

Chapter 6

Journal and Discussion Topics
1. What difficulties does Matthias encounter in getting Martin's sword?
2. If you were Log-a-Log or Matthias, what would you do when you realized Asmodeus was awake?

Summary
Log-a-Log holds the rock door open, and Matthias, looking in, sees a long dark tunnel sloping down. They call Guosim in whispers, but she doesn't answer, so Matthias leads the way down. When they are faced with 2 tunnels, they separate, ready to mark the tunnels so they can find their way back. Matthias soon finds an immense cavern that could hold the entire Great Hall of Redwall in a corner, when suddenly he hears the hissing noise, "Asmodeussssssss!" Terrified, he tries to calm himself, and begins looking for the snake. Entering the nearest cave, he spots Guosim, sitting with her back to the wall. Overjoyed, Matthias runs to her and grabs her paw, only to have her fall on her side, dead. It takes some time for Matthias to recover enough to continue his search for Asmodeus. Following a small tunnel, Matthias comes face to face with the sleeping viper. But, hanging from a tree root at the back of the den, Matthias spots the goal of his quest—the sword of Martin. Carefully, Matthias makes his way by Asmodeus, lifts down the sword, and feels that he and the sword are one. Matthias is ready to leave the cavern, but Asmodeus's tail lies across his path. He uses the point of the sword to tickle the tail, which causes Asmodeus to shift positions, and leaves Matthias a way out. As Matthias re-enters the main cavern, Log-a-Log races in, terrified, and yells to Matthias that Guosim is dead. His cry wakes Asmodeus.

Chapter 7

Journal and Discussion Topics
1. How do you explain the inclusion of Darkclaw in Cluny's dream?
2. What do you think Fangburn and Killconey will do now? What do you think they will tell Cluny?

Summary
Constance receives the news that the horde will emerge from the tunnel in the middle of the afternoon. Foremole is in charge of dealing with this threat. At the same time, Killconey is trying to convey to Cluny that the tunnel is ready, but Cluny is still responding abnormally. Killconey, Fangburn, and Darkclaw decide to try to carry on and keep Cluny's condition a secret. Killconey notes to the other commanders that they've run out of timber to shore up the entire tunnel, but he figures the army will move quickly enough to get through safely. A mole, listening in the Abbey grounds, hears every word Killconey says, and a report is given to Constance. The moles have lined up 2 huge cauldrons of boiling water to pour into the tunnel once the first rats emerge, and the Abbey inhabitants are grouped on the sides of a corded aisle. Under the commanders' guidance, the horde forms ranks, marches to the tunnel, and receives instructions from Fangburn about how they are to act when they emerge in the Abbey grounds: they are to capture the Abbot, open the gate, and subdue the Abbey fighters.

Meanwhile, Cluny is in his tent dreaming of the avenging warrior. In his nightmare, he is haunted by creatures that he killed in the past and his dead captains who urge him to face the warrior mouse. But Cluny runs away.

Darkclaw leads the breakthrough to the Abbey grounds, sees the lines of animals, and grins. But then he turns at a noise behind him, and faces the cauldrons of boiling water just as they are tipped over. Darkclaw is killed instantly. As soon as the cauldrons are tipped, Constance gives the order for the defenders to jump up and down between the ropes, and they cave in the tunnel. At the other end, Fangburn and Killconey are pushed aside as animals fight their way out.

The scene changes back to Cluny's dream, in which the dead Darkclaw now appears. Meanwhile outside Cluny's tent, Killconey and Fangburn argue over who should go in first to report the news to him. They finally decide that it is best not to disturb his sleep, as he might be having a nice dream.

Chapter 8

Journal and Discussion Topics

1. Do you think Asmodeus's death was fitting? Why or why not?
2. What did you think of the list of Matthias's reasons for striking Asmodeus?

Summary

Asmodeus sees that not only are there a shrew and a mouse invading his kingdom, but one of them holds a sword. Matthias doesn't yet see Asmodeus, but he realizes that they must escape quickly, so he seizes Log-a-Log and pulls him down a corridor . . . into a cul-de-sac. Log-a-Log is petrified, but Matthias quickwittedly uses the sword to dig a hole in the sandstone wall and urges Log-a-Log to climb through. Log-a-Log makes it, and grabs Matthias's feet to help him through, but as Log-a-Log begins to pull, Asmodeus arrives and bares his fangs. Log-a-Log manages to pull Matthias through the hole into the space behind, but Asmodeus thrusts his head through and Matthias quickly pushes Log-a-Log out of reach of Asmodeus's fangs. Asmodeus, however, is too large to come all the way through the hole—he becomes wedged in the wall. He tries to hypnotize Matthias with his eyes and voice. Matthias is succumbing, when suddenly Martin speaks to him, urging him to strike. Asmodeus is working himself free when Matthias breaks the hypnotic spell, raises the sword, and strikes Asmodeus blow after blow, until he has beheaded him.

mossflower woods

Quarry

the abbey

st. ninian's church

Vocabulary

A. Look at each expression. Tell what it means. Then tell who says it and why.

1. "kill two birds with one stone" (page 273)

   _____

2. "Give them back a taste of their own medicine!" (page 285)

   _____

B. Look at each group of words. Tell why it is important in the story.

1. plumage, regurgitating, orbs, macabre, preened

   _____

2. inferno, smoldering, holocaust, carnage, scorched

   _____

3. avenger, nemesis

   _____

4. cascaded, deluge, plummeting, cauldrons, tipstaves

   _____

5. trance, dilate, dominated, hypnotized, lethargy

   _____

Essay Topics

1. Read aloud the following portion of dialogue spoken by Log-a-Log (page 279) to find a pun. Then tell whether you think it was intentional or not and why. "Supposing the adder catches the scent of shrews? There's so many of us that it's a distinct danger."

2. Do you think the shrews' rules work well on the whole, or not? Explain your thoughts.

3. On page 294, the narrator says, "The young mouse knew that he had been born for this moment, his grip causing the tremor of the steel to run through his entire body. It was part of him!" We know that the sword isn't literally part of Matthias, so we might interpret this symbolically. What do you think it means?

4. Why do you think Jacques named the section you are reading "The Warrior"?

5. Respond to the following position: The existence of Asmodeus adds an interesting dimension to the plot: rather than being just a struggle between Cluny's horde and the inhabitants of Redwall, the story includes another unpredictable force that is harmful to both sides without differentiating. This makes the outcome of the war more unpredictable and adds suspense.

6. If you were Matthias, what would you do right now?

7. Now what role do you think the shrews will have in the rest of the story?

3-9

regiment	305 a number of battalions, each of which has 2 or more companies; similarly, each company has 2 or more platoons and each platoon has 2 or more squads
proffered	305 offered
armory	306 storehouse of weapons
inevitably	306 without question; unavoidably
disdainfully	306 proudly
clement	306 mild; pleasant
regimental	306 tyrannical; like a dictator
militaristic	306 shaped by military considerations
hubbub	307 uproar
priggishness	308 strict observance of what is proper
cress	308 watercress

3-10

fiasco	309 complete failure
respite	309 relief
cordage	309 ropes
devoid	310 without; lacking
fictitious	312 make-believe
vigilant	312 watchful; alert
amiss	313 wrong; out of the ordinary

3-11

remnants	314 remains; leftovers
truffle	314 edible fungus that grows underground
din	315 racket; hubbub
full complement	316 a complete group or number

3-12

bludgeoning	317 clubbing; beating
harried	317 bothered; overwhelmed with problems
homespun	317 homemade
drastic	318 extreme
laden	318 full of; burdened with
scum	319 rabble; worthless one

3-13

No vocabulary words

3-14

doom-laden	322 filled with a sense of dire destiny
complied	322 obeyed
dais	322 raised platform
fortitude	323 moral strength; courage
vengeance	323 revenge
consumed	323 eaten up
rending	323 tearing
convulsively	324 with violent spasms
hewed	325 cut; chopped
droves	325 swarms; flocks
teeming	325 present in large amounts
cloven	325 split
maelstrom	326 whirlpool
massacre	326 slaughter

besieged	326 plagued; attacked
stoically	326 apparently indifferent to feelings
throttle	327 strangle
vantage	328 view
bounty	331 the harvest

3-15

reprobate	333 unworthy one (here used in jest)
rambling	333 extending in an irregular way; not symmetrical

Chapter 9

Journal and Discussion Topics

1. What do you think of the advice Squire Julian gives Matthias about the sword? If you could add one thing, what would it be?
2. Name three incidents in this chapter that characters find surprising. .

Summary

The next afternoon, Matthias and the shrews return to the farm and meet Julian. Matthias shows Julian the blade, and Julian gives him some advice: the sword "will only be as good or evil as the one who wields it." Then they go to visit Captain Snow, who grudgingly returns the medal, makes the promise never to eat mice and shrews again, and apologizes to Squire Julian. But, against all expectation, Julian also apologizes and insists that the whole problem was his fault. Captain Snow insists on sharing the blame, and Julian invites him to lunch, observing that maybe the sword does have some magic after all. Matthias's laugh at this remark is echoed by the shrews, and the encounter ends joyfully for all.

Chapter 10

Journal and Discussion Topics

1. What do you think transformed Cluny back into his old self?
2. What would you have done if you were Plumpen? Explain your thinking.
3. Is your attitude toward people more like the Abbot's attitude (that there's some good in everyone) or like Jess's (that not everyone has good inside)? Explain your answer.

Summary

Cluny, returned to his old self, emerges from his tent, but uncharacteristically he gives his troops time to recuperate and refrains from berating them. During this respite, the gatehouse door is repaired from the damage caused by the battering ram. Cluny admires the work that, in his mind, is improving his future property, and sends Fangburn to light a large fire in the ditch. Then he has Mangefur and Scumnose bring the dormice and threatens to kill them unless Plumpen opens the Abbey door for him. Plumpen, faced with this choice, acquiesces to Cluny's demand. He slips into the Abbey workforce outside the walls, dressed in a habit taken from a dead Redwall resident, and steals into the Abbey with the other workers when their tasks are done. Plumpen is horrified by the betrayal he is about to commit, but when the time comes, he acts. While the other residents of the Abbey are resting after a booster speech by the Abbot, Plumpen hurries to the small north-wall gate, greases it, and opens it. Killconey carries word to Cluny. Plumpen waits for the horde to arrive, thinking that now his family will be safe, but even as this thought passes through his mind, Fangburn, at Cluny's instigation, clubs Plumpen on the back of the head. Cluny watches as the horde enters Redwall.

Chapter 11

Journal and Discussion Topics

1. What contrasts in mood did Jacques provide in this chapter for you?
2. Matthias believes he will have to face Cluny in single combat (one on one). What other examples of foreshadowing in the story suggest this?
3. What strategy(ies) would you suggest to the allies?

Summary

Matthias and the shrews are celebrating the death of Asmodeus and the safety of their species from Captain Snow and Julian, etc., when Log-a-Log mentions sparrows to Matthias, particularly one who is hanging around near the edge of the woods. Matthias gets Log-a-Log to go with him, and they head for Mossflower with about 20 shrews following. Soon Matthias finds the sparrow, and it turns out to be Warbeak, who is now queen of the Sparra. Warbeak tells Matthias that Cluny is inside Redwall. Log-a-Log, upon hearing the news, sends the shrews accompanying him back to prepare the army, while Warbeak, Matthias, and Log-a-Log set out as quickly as possible for Redwall.

Chapter 12

Journal and Discussion Topics

1. What changes have occurred in the way the horde operates? Do you find the changes believable? Why or why not?
2. How does Cluny interpret the words of his dream that "before sunset this day I would be free of my nightmares forever"? What other interpretations can you think of?
3. At this point in the story, what do you know that neither Cluny nor the imprisoned inhabitants of Redwall know?

Summary

Cluny takes the Abbot prisoner along with the Redwall captains, and has the Abbot's chair set up for himself. He renames the parts of the Abbey with titles reflecting his own taste and feelings. A rat pushes the Abbot for commenting that the dawn is coming, and is attacked by Jess, who is beaten for her efforts. By the time Cluny is going to come out and address them, the prisoners are completely demoralized.

Chapter 13

Journal and Discussion Topics

1. What additional details about the coming counterattack did you learn?
2. Would you treat Plumpen as a traitor? Why or why not?

Summary

Matthias leads Warbeak and Log-a-Log at a relentless pace, to the point where they finally pin him down and tell him he will collapse if he doesn't slow down. Log-a-Log decides to wait for the band of shrews. Matthias is worried about gaining entrance into the Abbey, but Warbeak says she will fly ahead and get the Sparras to open what she calls "little wormdoors in wall: east, south, north." At the same time, Plumpen awakes and opens his eyes to see 3 sparrows who promptly slide Plumpen out of one of the Abbey doors and into Mossflower Woods. Meanwhile, Dunwing has already given orders for the secret greasing of the hinges of the "little wormdoors." The Sparras, shrews, and Matthias all converge on Redwall.

Redwall: A Teaching Guide 73

Chapter 14

Journal and Discussion Topics

1. Do you have the sense that Abbott Mortimer is satisfied with his life and death? Explain.
2. What do you think of the Abbott's decisions about Matthias and Cornflower?
3. What unanswered questions do you have about the plot and the characters?
4. When did you realize that Matthias would live and Cluny would die? What led you to this conclusion?
5. How has the experience of the war with Cluny changed life for the defenders of Redwall and the woodlanders who helped them?

Summary

At dawn, Cluny makes a grand entrance, taking a seat in the Abbot's chair. Cluny calls Abbot Mortimer and asks him whether he will kneel and beg for his life. The Abbot refuses to kneel to someone "consumed by evil," and Cluny threatens to kill him. Constance wakes up and struggles in the net. She challenges Cluny to single combat, but Cluny has her beaten into unconsciousness. Basil then confronts Cluny, but a weasel smashes his legs with a club. Cluny then reminds the defenders of Redwall that he had given them an ultimatum to surrender or die at the beginning of the war, and now that he has won, he will kill them all. The Abbot rushes forward and pleads for them, but Cluny lashes the Abbot with the poison-barb on his tail, and declares that he will "Kill, kill, kill!" Suddenly the Warrior Mouse (Matthias) appears, proclaiming, "Cluny the Scourge, I have come to settle with you!" Cluny, terrified by this apparition, orders it to begone because he is not asleep. But the Warrior Mouse declares that he has come to fulfill the destiny of a preordained meeting with Cluny in single combat. The Joseph Bell begins to toll, and the Sparras and shrews launch an attack.

Cluny snatches a torch from Killconey and flings it at Matthias, who deflects it. Then Cluny shoves Killconey into Matthias and runs, but Matthias slays Killconey and follows. Fangburn sneaks up behind Matthias, but Constance intervenes, catching him in the net that once imprisoned her, and using it to swing him against the wall. Cluny tries to poison Matthias by lashing Matthias's face with his tail barb, but Matthias avoids him, and severs the end of Cluny's tail. Cluny throws the Abbot's chair at Matthias, then seizes an ironrailing spike and begins to fight. As the Sparras and other defenders keep up the battle, Matthias and Cluny continue their single combat. Cluny dashes into the Abbey and strikes at Matthias from behind the door. Matthias's sword gets lodged in the door, and Cluny is able to stab Matthias through the paw, while getting cut under the chin with Matthias's shield edge. While Cluny deals with his injury, Matthias recovers his sword, and they battle across to the entrance of the bell tower, where Friar Hugo, who had been tolling the Joseph Bell, runs under the stairs to escape Cluny. Cluny slams the door so that he and Matthias are locked in together. Cluny presses Matthias backward with the railing, attempting to choke him. Matthias suddenly swerves, throws himself down on his back, and kicks Cluny into the wall; then he leaps up and dashes up the stairs into the belfry. Cluny grabs Hugo and threatens to kill him unless Matthias throws down his sword and comes down. Matthias gives his word of honor that he'll come down, but only if Cluny releases Hugo first. Cluny agrees, glorying in the "knowledge" that the voices had been true and that he will soon "see the last of the warrior mouse." Matthias quickly severs the rope holding the Joseph Bell, which drops on Cluny, killing him instantly. Matthias comforts Hugo and goes out to the courtyard, where Constance and Basil tell him that not a single member of the horde still lives. Some rats unbarred the gate and tried to escape, but when they got outside they were met by a cat and an owl. Matthias is called to see the Abbot who is dying from the poison of Cluny's barb. The Abbot names Brother Alf as the next Abbot, gives a home to the Guerrilla Shrews at Redwall, and tells Matthias that he does not wish him to enter the Order of Redwall, but rather to be the Warrior Mouse of Redwall and defend the Abbey from evil and wrong. Abbot Mortimer then names the sword of the Abbey "Ratdeath." The Abbot calls Cornflower to him, tells her that he knows she will be a good wife to Matthias, and bequeaths them the old gatehouse as their home. Then he asks Constance to raise his head, and he tells his friends that he feels their friendship and love, and that just as the seasons come and go, he is going to a peaceful rest.

**Book Three
Chapter 15, Page 332**

Chapter 15

Journal and Discussion Topics

1. In what ways has the story come full circle?
2. All the evil characters in this book, except Sela (and maybe Killconey), are male. What do you think of this?
3. Were you satisfied with the ending? Why or why not?
4. Jacques has written both prequels (stories that come before) and sequels (stories that come after) *Redwall*. What would you expect to find in each?

Summary

This chapter picks up a year after the Abbot's death with a page from the *Annals* of Redwall recorded by John Churchmouse. Silent Sam has been heard speaking to Mattimeo, the son of Matthias and Cornflower. The new Abbot Mordalfus (Alf) has declared a feast for his firstyear anniversary, and Constance is out collecting the guests. The Guerrilla Shrews have made friends with the bees, and Queen Warbeak is a helper to Friar Hugo in the kitchen. Basil is out getting Captain Snow and Squire Julian for the feast, and Winifred and Ambrose Spike are testing the October ale to make sure it is good. Plumpen and his family are helping Foremole and his crew dig a roasting pit. Abbot Alf and Matthias have gone fishing in an attempt to bring back a larger fish than the one they caught last year. The Joseph Bell has been recast into 2 smaller bells: Matthias and Methuselah. The two little Churchmice, Tim and Tess, are the Abbey bellringers. The crops are growing well, and everything is beautiful at Redwall. The reader is invited to stop by and visit when he or she passes.

STRATEGY 11   Theme

Directions: Read the explanation, then answer the questions.

The **theme** of a story might be thought of as the story's point or its message. A theme is usually a generalization about life or human behavior or values, true, but not a truism—the author's insight into the way things work that s/he wants to share with readers. Theme is an important part of a story's meaning and is developed throughout the story. And it is important to note that a story can have multiple themes and meanings.

A persuasive or didactic piece of writing (such as a fable) might have an explicit moral—a clear statement of theme. Such a statement limits the interpretation of the piece. However, a piece of writing composed with experience or aesthetic response in mind is more open to interpretation. Certainly the author may have a theme or themes in mind, but the readers bring their own insights to bear on their understanding of the story. Therefore, different readers may legitimately find different meanings based on patterns and messages in the text combined with their own interpretations and insights.

The message is shaped by the author's intention and purpose. Besides patterns in the story (which often point to the theme), there are certain parts of a story that frequently refer to the theme: the title, the beginning, and the very end. An important character's first and final words are also likely to carry powerful indications of theme.

In a story, such as *Redwall*, which has a double plot—the story of Matthias's interior journey and the story of the war waged by Cluny—you may find multiple themes. But also try looking for a joining of the plots with a single, over-arching theme.

1. State the theme or themes you find as you finish reading the story. Explain how you concluded that these ideas are thematic.

STRATEGY 12

Rereading a Book

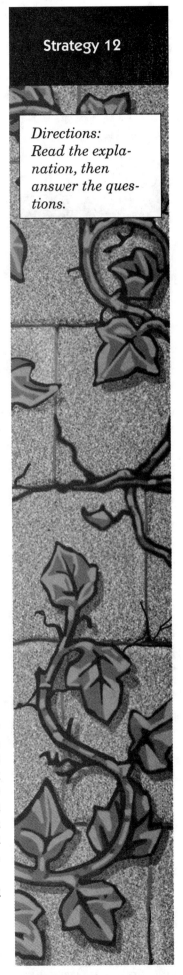

Directions: Read the explanation, then answer the questions.

Think of a book you've known for a while and read at least twice. How does your understanding of this book differ from the way you understand a book you've read only once?

- Do you remember details better?
- Do you remember the sequence of events better?
- Have you memorized parts of it?
- Can you imagine the characters in another setting?
- Do you return to the book when you feel or want to feel a certain way?
- Do you feel that all the parts of the book fit together to form a whole integrated experience?

Authors and critics alike suggest that reading fiction should be experiential. Novelist Joseph Conrad wrote, "My task, which I am trying to achieve, is, by the power of the written word, to make you hear, to make you feel—it is before all, to make you see. That, and no more, but it is everything." Janet Burroway, a writing instructor elaborates: "Written words are... at two removes from experience. .. They are transmitted first to the mind, where they must be translated into images... What it means is that... [the] fiction writer [must] focus attention, not on the words, which are inert, nor on the thoughts these words produce, but through these to felt experience, where the vitality of understanding lies." In other words, we don't read literature for information; we read it in order to pass through (in our minds) the sequence of events the author proposes, allowing our minds and hearts to respond to these events.

But all of this doesn't happen without the extended and complex act that we call reading. And in our first reading of a text, we cannot give ourselves fully to experiencing the story because we have to

- recognize black marks on the paper as letters and words
- process the words in groups to construct meaning and figure out how paragraphs and ideas are connected
- relate the perceived meaning to what we already know about stories in general, stories of the same genre as the one we're reading, earlier information from this particular story, etc.
- create in our minds the world of the story
- apply prior knowledge of facts, experiences, other stories, ideas, feelings, sensory data, etc., to help us understand what we have read
- try to recollect a new sequence of events and many facts and details
- fill gaps (no text tells absolutely everything) with our own elaborations

Considering the enormous investment of energy required to read, author Vladimir Nabokov said, "one cannot *read* a book: one can only reread it. . . . When we read a book for the first time the very process of laboriously moving our eyes from left to right, line after line, page after page, this complicated physical work upon the book, the very process of learning in terms of space and time what the book is about, this stands between us and artistic appreciation. . . . In reading a book, we must have time to acquaint ourselves with it. We have no physical organ (as we have the eye in regard to a painting) that takes in the whole picture and then can enjoy its details. But at a second, or third, or fourth reading we do, in a sense, behave towards a book as we do towards a painting."

Rereading is also important when we want to clarify, re-experience, or check on our understanding of a link between different parts of a book.

1. Reread *Redwall*. Keep track of how your second reading differs from your first reading. Note the differences and then try to characterize your second reading in terms of how you experienced the story.

Writer's Forum

In a book review, you identify the work by its title, author, and genre, give a summary leaving out some exciting details and the ending (so as not to spoil the book for others), and give your opinion of the work. You can begin in a fairly straightforward way with the background information: *Redwall* by Brian Jacques, the first of his animal fantasies, begins with a feast...

Or you could begin with the plot, for a different approach: It was the day of a great feast at Redwall Abbey. But little did the inhabitants know that . . .

Or you could begin with a question: Can the evil rat Cluny the Scourge and his horde of vermin defeat the good mice of Redwall Abbey and their woodland friends? This is the question the reader asks him- or herself as . . .

When you write the summary, it is a good idea to include the names of the main characters, the basic plot conflict, the setting, and the background of the situation. You usually should not include the climax or the crisis or the ending.

Your opinion statements should include your general feeling about the work as a whole and show how your reaction to elements of the work led you to that response. For example, you might respond positively because of the following:

- the plot is suspenseful and interesting
- the theme resonates with what you believe
- you like or admire one or more of the characters
- the vivid description catches your interest
- the book is amusing and enjoyable
- you learn something valuable
- you are so absorbed that you can't wait to read more
- you find insights or understandings that enrich your life

Your review does not have to include only your favorable responses, however. You may write an unfavorable review if you think, for example, that the

- dialogue is unrealistic
- the characterization is weak
- the characters' motivation are not believable
- the plot is convoluted or unbelievable
- the attitudes expressed seem inappropriate to you
- the genre doesn't appeal to you

It is also possible to present a situation in which you began with one point of view, but as your reading developed, your evaluation changed.

1. Write a book review sharing your opinion about the novel *Redwall*.

Writer's Forum

Compare and Contrast a Book and a Sound Recording

Sometimes you will want to compare and contrast two or more different treatments of the same subject in different genres or media. You might want to do this if a work has been adapted or translated to create a new work, if one work has inspired or influenced another work, or if they have the same subject and enough in common or such great disparities that you think it would be fruitful to see the similarities and differences in how they make meaning and achieve their effects.

In this particular case, you are going to contrast the book *Redwall* with the unabridged audiocassettes made of the book by Listening Library. It will be easier to do this if you have read the book twice, once to experience it and once to take notes for your paper, and if possible, before listening to the cassettes. Here are some questions that it would be useful to examine:

- Did the recording have any differences from the text that you could determine? Explain.
- What techniques were used in the recording to create characterization?
- How were your ideas of the characters' voices, behaviors, and "personalities" developed while reading the book similar to and different from the way they were presented in the audio recordings?
- What did the music add to the story of Redwall in the recording?
- Did the theme(s) you identified in the book come out in the recording? If not, what message(s) did the recording give?
- Apart from the book, did the recording work as an experience in itself? Did it hold your interest? Was it worthwhile?
- Which did you like better—the book or the recording? Why?

OperaDelaware has developed a musical version of *Redwall,* first presented in March 1998. If you have the opportunity to see the opera or the libretto, you can apply the above questions to the opera and you also might want to consider these additional questions:

- An opera is usually no longer than 2 hours, so an opera adaptation of a book leaves out material included in the book. What is excerpted or compressed in this opera?
- An opera libretto may have additional material not included in the book, or may make changes to the material in the book. What additions and/or changes do you notice?

Source words that can help you express concepts of similarity and difference include the following:

- as well as
- similarly
- differ
- whereas
- however

- likewise
- alike
- while
- but
- on the contrary

- at the same time
- resemble
- conversely
- though
- on the other hand

1. Write an essay comparing and contrasting the book and the recording of *Redwall.* Answer the questions listed above.

Vocabulary

Look at each group of words. Tell why it is important in the story.

1. regimental, militaristic, pompous

_____

2. remnants, epic, truffle

_____

Look at the expression. Tell what English expression it copies. Then tell what it means.

3. wing in paw (page 308)

_____

Essay Topics

1. How has Matthias changed since you met him on page 3?

2. Read the first sentence of every chapter. Then discuss the techniques Jacques uses to show the passage of time and give your reaction to them.

3 How has reading *Redwall* made a difference to you? What do you think you will remember most about it in the days ahead?

4. What was your reaction to the Abbot's last words (pages 330–331)?

5. Why do you think Jacques chose to end the book with an excerpt from the annals of Redwall?

6 What was your reaction to the climax of the story? Explain why you feel as you do.

7. What was your favorite part of the book? Tell why.

8. Do you plan to read another book in this series? Why or why not?

Answer Pages

Strategy 1: Beginning a Book, pages 12–13

Answers will vary. Allow for individual opinion.
1. Answers will vary. Students may not be able to go beyond the idea that the title names a place.
2. Answers will vary, depending on the edition students are using.
3. Answers will vary, depending on the edition students are using.
4. Number of years since 1986.
5. Students may be aware of other titles in the series.
6. Students may point out the Abbey setting, the search for something, and a war. Answers about illustrations will vary according to the edition used.
7. Students may identify the poem as a riddle and gather that there is an unknown hero and the genre is romantic fantasy.
8. Possible response: Matthias is mentioned first and seems to be the focus.
9. Possible responses: friendly; warm toward Matthias; trustworthy.
10. It takes place at Redwall Abbey, an imaginary setting, which is occupied only by animals (so far) and has a religious order, but is not overtly Christian, as one might expect.
11. Possible responses: talking animals; romantic mood; and setting.
12. The role of the warrior hero and whether Matthias can be one.
13. Answers will vary. Possible response: Matthias will face another obstacle to becoming a warrior.
14. Answers will vary.

Strategy 2: Map and Illustrations, page 14

1. Pictures of quarry, abbey, church, trees for Mossflower Woods.
2. The map shows a cat, an owl, and a snake. Possible response: They will be important characters in the story, and their particular location or habitat is important information.
3. Book One
    1. chess castle and illuminated animal
    2. warrior rat
    3. caught fish
    4. horse with bridle and blinders
    5. candles and hearts
    6. shield with skull and motto "Fur and Fang"
    7. moon and stars
    8. hooded warrior with face hidden holding a sword
    9. sun and fruit
    10. a strong door
    11. a building (the infirmary?)
    12. a tattered book
    13. sun rising behind abbey
    14. rats sneaking around at night
    15. rain falling and leaves blowing
    16. helmet, sword, shield, spear
    17. a hare; a shield and motto: stealthily
    18. a rat shot by an arrow ("Hate" is tattooed on his hand.)
    19. the gatehouse
    20. a ferret with a cutlass

Students should complete the list for Books Two and Three. For predictions, answers will vary. Students may predict that the book will contain adventures and battles.

Book One, Chapter 1, page 15

1. The Abbot is explaining to Matthias the role of the order.
2. Possible response: to provide sanctuary and assistance to the poor and needy.

3. To be a warrior hero. Students may or may not think that Matthias will achieve his goal. They may say that the existence of one warrior mouse (Martin) and the idea that there is a "bad guy" from the cover plus the picture of Matthias with a sword on the cover suggests that Matthias will become a warrior.
4. Possible response: The textual evidence so far suggests that Matthias would need to grow a lot in maturity and vision to become a leader like Martin. The picture on the cover suggests that whatever deficits of character Matthias has now, he will be able to overcome them in order to achieve a stature like Martin's.
5. Possible response: The Abbot's first response as suggested by the narrator—"What a young buffoon of a mouse"—suggests condescension and impatience. By the end of the chapter, the Abbot's response is benign and sympathetic, and he has made an effort to provide a way for Matthias to have a sense of achievement.

Book One, Chapter 2, page 15
1. Students may find that it's unclear whether the rat in the picture is Cluny based on the verbal description.
2. Answers will vary. Students illustrations should show characteristics mentioned in the text, e.g., ragged fur, curved teeth, black eyepatch.
3. Possible response: Cluny will be matched against Matthias—the character who seems like he'll be the hero.
4. Many students may predict that he will end up at the Abbey.
5. Answers will vary. Possible response: Maybe Cluny has his followers pay him homage as if he were a God.
6. Possible responses: The Abbey may become a refuge for those fleeing from Cluny; Matthias may be called upon to defend the Abbey from Cluny.
7. Answers will vary. Answers should take into account the characteristics of the horse and the rats and Cluny.

Strategy 3: Animal Fantasy/Proper Names, page 16
1. **Good:** mice, otters, hedgehogs, squirrels, voles, badgers, hare, moles, shrews, sparrows, cat, owl. **Bad:** rats, weasels, stoats, ferrets, snake, foxes.
2. Sample answers: Jess Squirrel: climbing roof; rappeling. Moles: tunneling.
3. Students may find that some names refer to something that reflects the goodness or evil of the character: Cornflower, Constance, on the one hand; Skullface, Killconey, Cheesethief, on the other hand; or simply physical traits, such as Dunwing. Some names may recall historical figures, especially saints or Old Testament figures (Martin, Ambrose, Matthias, Methuselah, Basil, Julian, John, Abram, Colin). Guosim is an acronym; Log-a-Log is an occupation; Cluny is the name of a monastery in France; Silent Sam names a character trait; Jess, Tess, Alf, and Tim may seem to be just ordinary names.

Book One, Chapter 3, page 17
1. Catching the enormous fish with Brother Alf. He receives praise from the cook, Friar Hugo; praise from Winifred, the otter who is a champion at fishing; thanks from the Abbot.
2. Possible responses: saying grace; helpers making people welcome; guests praising the appearance of the main course; guests taking places assigned to them.
3. Possible response: It lets the reader know that Redwall could withstand a siege if Cluny attacks the Abbey.
4. His concentration on her physical beauty lets the reader know that he is attracted to her.

Book One, Chapter 4, page 17
1. Possible response: Cluny is a tyrant who leads by intimidation rather than by example or inspiration.
2. Possible response: He is guided by an evil impulse or possibly by an actual evil spirit, depending on how the third sentence is interpreted.
3. Possible response: Cluny will attack Redwall; Matthias will assume the role of Warrior to defend the Abbey and will defeat Cluny.

Book One, Chapter 5, page 18
1. A gift of food, given in a way so as not to cause offense.
2. They begin to know each other as they join in caring for the two baby churchmice. Then, as Constance gives them a ride home, Cornflower falls asleep against Matthias's shoulder. Brother Alf's remarks suggest that at some point Matthias will have to choose between Cornflower and his vocation at Redwall.

3. Possible responses: that unusual events will take place this summer; that things now dormant or in the budding state (like Matthias's desire to be a warrior or the relationship between Matthias and Cornflower) will develop and come into their own as the book progresses.
4. To report to the Abbot.
5. Possible response: They might have been on the path in the way of the hay cart when it came hurtling past, and so been injured, killed, or taken prisoner.

Book One, Chapter 6, page 18
1. Possible responses: He is quick to respond to situations; invigorated by danger; contemptuous of those who are not as courageous and strong as he is; rude; evil; a confident leader; a strategist and tactician.
2. Cluny says he wants to find a better place to stay than St. Ninian's. He sends scouts to find a better place to stay, and tells them to look for "a big place," by which he seems to mean the Abbey.
3. He sends out scouts and a press-gang to recruit animals that know the area.
4. The architectural features that can serve as weapons.
5. Possible response: that Cluny is settling into the area and will be carrying out some kind of operation here.
6. Possible response: The Abbot mentions physical characteristics of animals as part of a prayer, showing reverence for the different aspects of creation. The caption seems to be a motto of war, and the reference to "fang" where the Abbot says "tooth" emphasizes predation rather than the enjoyment of food at a feast.

Strategy 4: Setting: Redwall Abbey, page 19
Help students see the pattern of alternating settings as the narrative moves between Redwall and Cluny's camp at St. Ninian's, and the change to a single setting when Cluny attacks Redwall. Students should also attend to the particular settings that are proper to the shrews, Julian, Captain Snow, and Asmodeus, and the relationship between setting and character in these cases.

Book One, Chapter 7, Page 20
1. Possible response: that the action takes place during the night.
2. Possible responses: eyewitness testimony; authoritative sources; collaborated information; sixth sense; traveler's tales; records; personal integrity.
3. Possible response: He has access to a wealth of valuable information; he has the gift of tongues; he has a wonderful memory for past events; he is wise and truthful.
4. A mine disaster, burning a farmhouse, eating piglets alive, spreading sickness and disease among livestock, stampeding a herd of cows.
5. Possible responses: They don't want to believe it, or they're afraid to believe it, or they're used to thinking of Cluny as a legend rather than a real threat.
6. Answers will vary. Possible responses: He will prepare to defend Redwall; he will make preparations to go out and confront Cluny. Students may note that the Abbot and Matthias perhaps have different ideas of what they're getting ready for. Matthias is more likely to be getting ready to fight, while the Abbot may think of getting ready to provide food, safety, and medical treatment to those affected by Cluny's advance Students may mention making sure of an adequate food and water supply; developing a tactical approach; finding weapons; making a place for those who dwell outside the Abbey but who may need to seek refuge there.
7. It seems to require the response of a warrior.

Book One, Chapter 8, page 20
1. Answers will vary. Students may think it is an evil figure or they may think it is the guardian of the sword shown on the cover of the book.
2. The phantom figure from Cluny's dream. Some students may guess that it is Matthias as the warrior he will become.
3. He gives them false signals (e.g., in facial expression) about his emotions in order to lull them into a sense of security; then he punishes them.
4. He uses intimidation, threats, and terror to ensure obedience.

Strategy 5: Plot Conflict, page 21

1. Students may identify Matthias's desire to become a great warrior like Martin—which involves external conflicts such as overcoming the Abbot's opposition and finding the armor and sword of Martin, as well as the internal conflict Matthias faces in needing to overcome his own immaturity. They may identify the struggle between Cluny's forces and the Redwall contingent as another conflict, related to the first, yet separate.
2. Students should recognize the episodic nature of the plot and identify the conflict or conflicts in each chapter.
3. Students should be able to identify and discuss the way that Jacques moves back and forth from one locus to the other.

Strategy 6: Point of View, page 22

1. So far students may find passages that reflect the inner thoughts of Matthias, the Abbot, Skullface, Cluny, and Cornflower.
2. He is omniscient and speaks of the events in the third person—he is not involved in the story himself. He seems to know the story and knows what will happen next before it happens, and he knows the characters' thoughts, sometimes speaking in the characters' voice. For example, on page 29, when the narrator says, "Their assumption was correct," he is asserting his omniscient knowledge of Cluny's true mood. But when he says, "The Chief was in a good mood," he is expressing Ragear and Mangefur's (false) assumption from their point of view.

Book One, Chapter 9, page 23

1. The Abbot believes that Redwall will be saved from Cluny by a miracle. Constance believes that miracles are a thing of the past.
2. Answers will vary. Students may focus on Matthias's potential or the changes he has to undergo.
3. Answers will vary. Students may point out that this kind of animal grouping can be found in other works and Jacques is following a tradition. They may also feel that this division is arbitrary.
4. Answers will vary. Students expectations should be reasonably based on the material characterizing Cluny and the Redwall inhabitants so far.

Book One, Chapter 10, page 23

1. Possible responses: The sight of the armed horde with himself at its head, and reading the articles to the defenders of Redwall, in other words, fear; using a parley to get inside Redwall and noticing the arrangement of the buildings, etc.; testing the Redwall soldiers' courage and discovering that they are "untrained and untested"; giving an ultimatum.
2. Possible responses: Cluny has stated their ideal accurately. Constance's words when she picked up the table show that she might have been willing to break the rule of hospitality in pressing circumstances, so Cluny's estimation may be too simplistic.
3. Possible responses: Matthias feels it is an error to have let Cluny see that the Redwall defenders are not trained; it may have been an error to have the parley in Cavern Hole rather than in the courtyard because Cluny got to see more of the Abbey; Cluny thinks it was a strategic error to have lost the element of surprise.
4. Possible response: It could be symbolic of how depraved he is, that he doesn't like something that most everyone would agree is delicious.
5. Possible responses: Maybe Martin isn't really dead. Maybe Martin's ghost will return. Maybe the similarities Methuselah observed between Matthias and Martin are confusing Cluny, and it is really Matthias about whom he is dreaming. Maybe it is a foreshadowing of what will happen later in the novel: single combat between Cluny and a mouse.

Strategy 7: Plot—The Design of a Story, page 24

1. Students may identify the 3 parts of the story as connecting to the beginning, the middle, and the end. How they identify the crisis and climax may depend on whether they see the main conflict as Matthias's quest for identity as a warrior or the struggle between good (as represented by Redwall) and evil (as represented by Cluny and his horde). Many students may identify Book One, Chapter 10, as the beginning of the complication, when Cluny formally confronts the Abbot. Students are likely to identify the climax as the fight between Matthias and Cluny.

Strategy 8: Foreshadowing and Flashback, page 25

1. Students may refer to the riddle on page xiv, especially "Take on my mighty role," and "Look for the swords" coupled with the title of Book Two, "The Quest," as being foreshadowing. They may identify one or more of the following—Matthias's wish to be a warrior, the title of Book Three, "The Warrior," and Cluny's dream of a warrior mouse—as foreshadowing as well.

Test 1: Book One, Chapters 1–10, page 26

Vocabulary
1. These are the names of roles within the Abbey of Redwall.
2. These are words that characterize the members of Cluny's horde.
3. These are words that describe the role that Redwall Abbey has by virtue of the beliefs of the order of Redwall mice.

Essay Topics
1. Students' reflections and revised predictions should be based on the new knowledge they have gained through reading Chapters 1–10.
2. Answers will vary depending on the book chosen. In *The Wind and the Willows,* for example, Ratty, the water rat (along with Mole, Toad, and Badger) is one of the heroes, while the stoats and weasels are among the villains. In *Mrs. Frisby and the Rats of NIMH,* there are mice and rats working together, and though some individual rats are traitors, it is not linked to the species but to individual choice.
3. Students should pick a story that in some way resembles *Redwall.* For example, students could make a comparison with the beginning of *The Three Musketeers,* when D'Artagnan is seeking to become a warrior but has not yet had the opportunity, and many think he is not up to the role. Or they might find similarities with *The Hobbit,* when Bilbo has a role in the dwarves' quest but it seems as if he will have to undergo a lot of development in order to fulfill his role.
4. Students' favorite moments will vary. They should give support for their answers.
5. Students' favorite characters will vary. They should give support for their answers.
6. Students' rewrites should consistently represent the identified narrator's point of view, being limited to what s/he could reasonably know and representing within reason what the character would be likely to feel and think.
7. Possible responses: his management style; his feelings interfere with his reason; he's evil; he is too sure of the power of fear to coerce others.
8. Answers will vary. Possible responses: Matthias should have already known everything the Abbot told him before he joined the order of Redwall; Cornflower needs more personality; some of the dialogue is stilted.

Book One, Chapter 11, page 29

1. By reaching Ambrose from underground, they avoided a possible ambush above ground.
2. They make calculations; they discuss the technical requirements of this specific tunnel; they do a test of the ground and report back to Foremole; the tunnel holds so that they are able to quickly rescue Ambrose and bring him within the Abbey walls.
3. Martin's sword was magic.
4. Because she can recognize Matthias's gifts and abilities, she gives him the support and encouragement he needs in his continued desire to become a warrior.
5. Matthias's reason for wanting to rescue them is that they face certain death or slavery. Constance's reason against the rescue is that a few Redwall inhabitants cannot take on the hundreds of rats available to guard the Voles, so the rescuers would probably end up dead.

Book One, Chapter 12, page 29

1. Possible response: Cluny's evil nature is highlighted against the backdrop of St. Ninian's.
2. It's not clear what species he is; Cluny sometimes shows more respect to him than to other horde members; he has climbing ability beyond any other beast.
3. Possible response: I thought he wanted to have him open the gate.
4. Martin is so important to the Redwall community that the loss of the tapestry will destroy their morale. Possible response: He might want it in order to try to understand his nightmare better.

5. Answers will vary. Possible response: It might actually have the opposite effect—that of uniting their opposition to him.

Book One, Chapter 13, page 30

1. Possible responses: that Cluny will besiege the Abbey so they will need food for a long time; that they will fight, but only to defend themselves.
2. They now tease each other and are more familiar.
3. Possible responses: He can see Matthias's thoughts in his face. He is able to anticipate Matthias's train of thought, perhaps because it is similar to his own.
4. Students may or may not think that the sparrowhawk's story is a valuable clue.

Book One, Chapter 14, page 30

1. Students may disagree, either because they believe that combating evil is everybody's business or because they see the world as one community in which everyone must take responsibility for each other.
2. Possible responses: **D:** "the hot dry day, damping down the dust from the road" (page 59). **S:** "Ever upwards, sometimes stopping spreadeagled against the surface" (page 60).
3. Cluny doesn't understand his nightmare; it frightens him; it contains Martin, but as a figure of vengeance. Matthias recognizes his dream as a call to action; he is not afraid, but only puzzled at first to understand the message; Martin appears as a friend in need.
4. Answers will vary. Students may think that the mice will be devastated or moved to united action.
5. Students may think that he rejoins the horde later.
6. As Cluny explained in Chapter 12 (pp. 52—53), one alone could not attack the gatehouse and open the gate. Shadow is, Cluny thinks, likely to be able to get the tapestry, which the mice honor extremely, and he believes its loss will demoralize them and throw them into confusion.

Strategy 9: Characterization, page 31

1. The moles' dialect; their act of saving Ambrose and the other characters' words in admiration of how they did it; the cooperation shown in their interactions.
2. Students' responses will vary.
3. Possible responses: she thinks quickly, states her case strongly, feels able to reinforce her position with action, shows her emotions.
4. Possible response: Matthias is growing into the role of Abbey Warrior.
5. Possible response: Methuselah is like a guide and helper to Matthias in his search, and like a guardian of knowledge for Redwall—in a way, like a wizard.

Book One, Chapter 15, page 32

1. The grey skies and rain reflect the subdued atmosphere of the Abbey inhabitants.
2. Students may agree that the leader must inspire followers whatever s/he feels or they may think that honesty is important.
3. Methuselah doesn't realize that Matthias is also hiding his true feelings, and his plans, from him.
4. It increased his confidence.

Book One, Chapter 16, page 32

1. He wants dominion over every living creature.
2. Possible response: Although the Vole family does not have liberty, they still have and exercise freedom.

Book One, Chapter 17, page 33

1. Basil takes personal responsibility for the whole countryside in which he lives, and for this reason is willing to get involved in the struggle against Cluny.
2. Students may think he will be hurt because he cannot control himself, or that he will mature.
3. Students may think that the others would not have let Matthias go if he'd told them, or that it is irresponsible, during a war especially, to leave without letting someone know.
4. Students may think that they'll escape, possibly with Basil's help.

Book One, Chapter 18, page 33

1. **Cluny:** stays out of range; uses the sling throwers to stop the archers; uses scaling ladders and grappling hooks with ropes to ascend the wall; uses the sling throwers again when the Redwallers are off guard. **Redwall:** uses arrows to disconcert the horde; uses rubble to knock down the scaling ladders and beavers to sever the ropes.
2. Possible response: He will do harm to whoever crosses his path, regardless of their allegiance, and so unknowingly and without concern hurt one side and help the other and vice versa.
3. Possible response: It seems like a good strategy.
4. Cluny can be proactive, while the defenders are limited, to a certain extent, to reacting to what Cluny does.

Writer's Forum: Dialogue, page 34

Students should write dialogue that seems appropriate to the characters they choose and to the situation of the encounter. The dialogue should be correctly punctuated.

Writer's Forum: Description, page 35

Students may choose to use the suggested categories for describing Basil. They should include a description of his language as well. Students may describe Cluny's dream primarily in terms of the feelings Cluny experiences and the visual characteristics of the phantom.

Book One, Chapter 19, page 36

1. He doesn't want to leave his wife and son captive.
2. Basil's disappearance at an awkward time; his manner when he reappears; his explanation of his absence.
3. Answers will vary.
4. Possible responses: He is tired; he is lying down; the soothing sound of the river; it is warm.

Book One, Chapter 20, page 36

1. He criticizes them for not having characteristics that they don't have by nature, and which he didn't consider in choosing them for the assignment. He criticizes Cheesethief for discovering something he probably never had the opportunity to discover before.
2. Students may or may not appreciate the descriptions.
3. The rock catapult, the rat javelins, and the iron grave-railings tied to cord.
4. Possible response: They might run out of ammunition such as arrows, boulders, and pebbles.
5. Instead of being positive for Cluny and negative for Redwall, it seems it will be positive for Redwall.
6. It is a reference to the song "Baa, Baa Black Sheep" and refers to the sheeps' slavish answer to the master.

Test 2: Book One, Chapters 11–20, page 37

Vocabulary
1. These are some of the moles' considerations in rescuing Ambrose.
2. These are some of Basil's expressions.
3. These are parts of the Church of St. Ninian.

Essay Topics
1. Possible responses: **Cluny's Horde:** Cluny's leadership style; lack of middle-level management; tension between species. **Redwall:** the difference in various animals' ideas of whether Redwall should only defend or conquer Cluny; lack of leadership; individuality (for example, Matthias's choice to leave without telling) over unity.
2. Students should refer to the methods of characterization given on page 31.
3. Answers will vary depending on the choice of book. Possible choices include *The Iliad, The Hobbit, Watership Down,* and *Over Sea, Under Stone.*
4. Students should support their answers.
5. At first the chapters would be about either Cluny or about Redwall. Now that they are involved in a battle, he moves back and forth between camps within a chapter. Possible response: The chapter structure thus mirrors the plot.

6. Answers will vary depending on the animals chosen. Elements they might point out: **Basil:** affectation and British usages; **Killconey:** Irish accent and many questions; **Moles:** lower-class dialect and usages (e.g., "bide") that seem archaic to a modern ear.

Book Two, Chapter 1, page 40

1. Students may be surprised that the noise turns out to be a baby squirrel, or that the squirrel can help Matthias find his way back.
2. Possible responses: enjoyment of nature; self-loathing; despair; fear; courage; relief; trust; joy.
3. Answers will vary. Some students may believe that both in leaving without telling and in allowing himself to fall asleep, Matthias is blameworthy. Other students may think his actions are understandable and forgiveable, given his aim.

Book Two, Chapter 2, page 40

1. He is making a kind of joke; perhaps he wants to lighten the mood or show his usefulness.
2. Possible responses: **Yes:** He knows what he can do himself and what he should delegate, and to whom; **No:** His opinion that Cluny would not trouble them again is not founded in reality.
3. Because Cluny has more regard for Scragg, a weasel, than for Cheesethief, a rat, and because Scragg is very capable and shows up Cheesethief in maneuvering the plank.
4. Possible response: probably not from Cluny, who doesn't know what happened, but it would seem that such an evil character would get some punishment in a story about good and evil.
5. Possible response: It might add support to Matthias's view that Cluny's evil horde must not just be repelled, but must be overthrown once and for all.
6. Cowl over tail = head over heels; grinning from whisker to tail = grinning from ear to ear; single-pawed = single-handed; mousekind = humankind.
7. The Abbot is more democratic, listens to his followers, and discerns who is best equipped for each role in Redwall's defense. Cluny is tyrannical, usually initiates and supervises everything himself, and doesn't always choose appropriate personnel for a mission.
8. Students may predict that Cluny will die; that he will live but be killed eventually by the phantom mouse; etc.

Book Two, Chapter 3, page 41

1. Students may think of vitality as being positive and so be struck by the phrase.
2. In the first dream, Cluny is carrying out his evil designs, when the phantom mouse appears, pursues him, and is killing him with a sword when Cluny awakes. The second dream opens with his fall from the plank; then he sees Ragear, a rat skeleton in his own armor, a hare, and a snake, before he encounters the phantom mouse who again is killing him with the sword when he awakes.
3. Possible response: He is concerned that a fox might want to eat him.
4. Cluny's—it shows his point of view.

Book Two, Chapter 4, page 41

1. Possible responses: to give readers time to puzzle over it before the answers began to be revealed; to give some hints about the plot; to raise questions about the plot and increase suspense.
2. He looks at the riddle a little at a time; he assumes that what the riddle says is true, even if it seems contrary to fact; he thinks out loud with a partner; he pays attention to the structure of the riddle and the punctuation; he goes to the locations the riddle seems to indicate.
3. Answers will vary. Possible responses: Try to read it out loud; look at the context and at what others ask or reply to the moles; use Methuselah's translation.
4. The tomb of Martin, because the poem says that is where the Warrior sleeps.

Writer's Forum: Summary, page 42

1. Students' summaries should focus on strategies as the main details.

Writer's Forum: Riddles, page 42
1. Students' riddles should show clever connections between an object and another object or between an object and a description.

Book Two , Chapter 5, page 43
1. Possible response: **Sela:** Though the narrator says that Cluny can see through her dancing and trickery (page 125), he then says that Cluny wouldn't have slept if he had known what she was really up to (page 126), and she does succeed in sending a message out to the Abbot.
2. Answers will vary. Possible response: The Abbot would refer the matter to Constance and Matthias.
3. Students may believe that if Cluny can see through Sela's dancing, sooner or later he will see through her other deceptions.

Book Two, Chapter 6, page 43
1. Answers will vary.
2. Possible response: The pattern seems to fit, and Matthias is strengthened in his mission as Warrior by the possession of the sword belt and shield, as well as by the familiar feel of the shield and the new poem.
3. They do not look like objects that have been unused for a long time.
4. It is a way to find the sword.

Book Two, Chapter 7, page 44
1. She seems to be planning an ambush.
2. Come here.
3. Answers will vary. Students may think that Constance's help was needed, or that they eventually would have figured it out.
4. Answers will vary. Students may mention the value of community effort.

Book Two, Chapter 8, page 44
1. Cluny spied on Sela, got information from Fangburn, secretly stopped taking the medicine that made him sleep, pretended to sleep, made an elaborate plan of attack that was not his main plan and left it out so Sela would find it and think it was a great piece of good fortune that she got to see it.
2. Possible response: He connects his strategic ability to an ability to play chess really well.

Book Two, Chapter 9, page 45
1. Possible response: She had invaded their territory.
2. Possible response: She is courageous, angry, defiant.
3. Answers will vary. Possible response: Maybe the sparrows moved it.

Book Two, Chapter 10, page 45
1. Possible response: Because she knows he is playing with her and could kill her easily.
2. Sela, Fangburn, and Redtooth betray Cluny's trust; Constance betrays Sela's trust; Cluny tricks Sela, but this is not betrayal.
3. Answers will vary. Possible response: They know that they cannot escape from him, so they feel that they have no choice.

Test 3: Book Two, Chapters 1-10, page 46
Vocabulary
1. These are things Sela uses to cure Cluny.
2. These words describe aspects of the roof that Jess climbs.
3. These words describe how Silent Sam acts with the knife that Basil gives him.

Essay Topics

1. Answers should include the following ideas: After initial setbacks, including major injury to himself, Cluny has succeeded in duping the Redwallers into thinking his next invasion plan is to use a battering ram on the front gate while he is actually concentrating his efforts on tunneling under the wall. The Redwall inhabitants may think they have the information they need to defend against Cluny's next attack, but they have been tricked and are vulnerable.
2. Answers will vary depending on the traitor. Possible choices include Edmund in *The Lion, the Witch and the Wardrobe,* Jenner in *Mrs. Frisby and the Rats of NIMH,* Mordred in the legends of King Arthur, Blodwen Rowlands in *The Silver on the Tree.*
3. Answers will vary. Possible response: **Yes:** They have no way of knowing that Cluny set Sela up.
4. Answers will vary.
5. Answers will vary. Students may feel satisfied that the promised confrontation has taken place, or they may feel disturbed by the violence.
6. Answers will vary. The dialogue should reflect the characters' personality traits, attitudes, and characteristic ways of speaking.
7. Students may note that strange and unexpected encounters occur in Mossflower.

Book Two, Chapter 11, page 50

1. Answers will vary. Possible responses: If the Redwallers continue only to defend themselves, they will eventually run out of supplies and be defeated, in which case their mission will fail; or the new stance is clearly against Redwall's mission to feed the hungry, care for the sick and injured, and provide sanctuary—they should continue in their mission whatever the cost.
2. Repetition and exclamations show a one-track mind and a temper. Her topic makes her seem bloodthirsty and vengeful.

Book Two, Chapter 12, page 50

1. Contradiction in direction of the noise; Fangburn's injuries are not consistent with bumping into a thorn bush; Fangburn almost agrees with Cluny's sarcastic remark about flying pigs; Sela has returned without the herb.
2. Students' affective responses to Asmodeus will differ.
3. Eternity refers to life after death or the afterlife. It is a poetic way of saying that Redtooth is going to die because Asmodeus is going to eat him.

Book Two, Chapter 13, page 51

1. Students may feel that Matthias is overly violent, or that he uses the only methods that will work with such a defiant prisoner.
2. Possible response: These tensions may divide the horde so that it loses some of its effectiveness.
3. The words he uses in response to Cluny's question: shoring, banking, sinking shafts, galleries.
4. Possible response: They will be killed.

Book Two, Chapter 14, pages 51–52

1. She saves Matthias's life.
2. Answers will vary. Possible responses: make him work for them; kill him.

Book Two, Chapter 15, page 52

1. He is disgusted with what he now considers her inept attempts to outsmart Cluny.
2. Students may feel that the Abbot's disassociation from violence and commitment to helping others are phony, since he encourages or allows those under his authority to violate his principles.
3. He is at first suspicious and dispassionate and allows Jess to question Chickenhound's motivation. When he is satisfied that Chickenhound came to give them information, he orders him taken to the infirmary, and tells Chickenhound that he will care for him, whether or not he gives them information.
4. His goal seems to be to ransack Redwall Abbey. He has gotten within the Abbey, with a reason to remain there for some time, and gained the Abbot's confidence by sharing information about Cluny's planned attack.

Book Two, Chapter 16 , pages 52–53

1. Possible responses: that the king is unpredictable, impulsive, dangerous, and tyrannical, and that he can make Bull Sparra believe that he's a mouse who is weak in the head.
2. They are both tyrannical and violent.
3. They are both classified as legends by those who have not had personal experience with them.
4. Answers will vary. Students may predict that because Book Three is called "The Warrior," Matthias will escape and help save Redwall. They may conjecture that an alliance with Dunwing, who has reason to be upset with Bull Sparra and possibly has the power to actively help Matthias, is a possibility.

Writer's Forum: Compare and Contrast, page 54

Students should mention that sharing food increases community at Redwall; that Cluny does not like Redwall food (the milk and honey); and that food creates dissension in Cluny's horde.

Book Two, Chapter 17, page 55

1. To hearten the Abbot and the troops and to dishearten Cluny and his horde.
2. Students may think that Cluny always had this attitude, or that he has deepened his resolve.
3. Students should cite evidence about Cluny from pages 204–206 and about the Abbey training from pages 55–56.
4. Possible response: the beginning of the end for Cluny.
5. Answers will vary.

Book Two, Chapter 18, page 56

1. Dunwing has identified the escape route, arranged to have Jess come to meet Matthias and help him descend, and created a plan to get the other sparrows out of the way so that Matthias can both steal the sword belt and scabbard and escape.
2. King Bull Sparra could take the sword belt and scabbard with him—since he is going to think he is about to recover the sword, this would make sense. Some sparrows might stay behind or they might not be gone long enough for Matthias to complete his escape. They might not believe the lie.
3. Answers will vary. Students may predict that one or both of them die. Possible response: Matthias falls on Bull Sparra, cushioning his fall. Bull Sparra is killed on impact.

Book Two, Chapter 19, page 57

1. Possible response: Since it didn't serve a purpose in his plans, perhaps he did it just because he "enjoyed" destroying things.
2. If he had left everything looking as normal as possible, so that the thefts wouldn't be detected; if he hadn't booted open the door to the kitchen but gone quietly; if he had avoided Methuselah rather than killing him; if he had planned his escape, so that when Constance came after him, he didn't have to make the choice at hand.
3. Answers will vary. Students may recognize that people's actions give meaning to their lives and deaths.
4. Answers will vary. Many students may be surprised that he was found in that way or at that time. Students who have relied on the Book titles, who understand the meaning of the riddle and/or Cluny's dream will expect Matthias to be found alive.

Book Two, Chapter 20, page 58

1. They are probably terrified of angering Cluny or making any mistake.
2. He hopes to terrify them so that they will submit more easily.

Book Two, Chapter 21, page 58

1. Possible response: that Matthias must get the sword from Asmodeus, but the encounter will be dangerous.
2. Answers will vary. Students may feel that Basil is right—that Matthias has grieved enough–or that he is insensitive to Matthias's feelings.
3. Not very—he doesn't act like he's really wounded.
4. Answers will vary. Students may feel that Matthias's sense of his mission guides his decisions well or that he is again being irresponsible.

Book Two, Chapter 22, page 59

1. He becomes more deferential and apologetic and careful in his explanation. Answers will vary: He may change because he realizes he is taking part in an orderly meeting where respect is mandated—not a free for all.
2. Possible responses: impulsive, disorderly, touchy, violent, democratic.
3. Answers will vary. Possible response: He will hold the cat's mouth open.

Book Two, Chapter 23, page 59

1. Students may feel an increase of suspense.
2. Answers will vary. Students may suggest various schemes for limiting the damage or making it impossible to use.
3. Answers will vary. Students may suggest filling it with a substance that will hurt the rats.

Strategy 10: Imaging, page 60

1. Images and the quality of the students' drawings will vary. They should portray elements of the story with detail and understanding.

Test 4: Book Two, Chapters 11–23, page 61

Vocabulary
1. Crazy; Constance doesn't understand Matthias's investment of time and energy in Warbeak.
2. Talk without accompanying action; the narrator is telling secondhand the mice's opinion of Basil.
3. Move your legs faster; Basil is telling one of the Brothers to walk more quickly.
4. An older person can be the most foolish of all; the narrator is telling secondhand Chickenhound's opinion of the Abbot.
5. As secretive as robbers; the narrator is describing the private talks between Basil and Jess.
6. Those who help you when you are in need are really your friends; the narrator is telling secondhand Matthias's view of Dunwing and Warbeak.
7. Very chancy; Cornflower is describing how critical Matthias's condition was through the night.
8. Took away their motive power; Basil is analyzing the first attack.

Essay Topics
1. Students should point out that Cluny's plan is more coherent and better carried out, and strategically better calculated to overthrow Redwall. They should support their observations with details from the text.
2. Answers will vary. Students should defend their opinions with reasons.
3. Given the riddle, students are likely to think that Matthias will regain the sword. If they understand Cluny's dream, they may understand that the sword will cause Cluny's death.
4. It is largely occupied by Matthias's search for Martin and his armor. Students should detail the quest.
5. Students may feel more sympathy for Sela than for Chickenhound. They should describe their reactions with some detail.
6. Answers will vary. Possible responses: upset, disconcerted, concerned, annoyed, etc. Students should follow their analysis with a response.
7. Answers will vary. Students should base their predictions on a realistic assessment of what the shrews can or might be able to do.

Book Three, Chapter 1, page 64

1. Answers will vary. Students' answers should be at least somewhat realistic. For example, drive bent spikes into the battering ram to use as handles.
2. Answers will vary. Students should support their opinions with details.
3. They both have inflated opinions of themselves that lead to their demise. Students should support their analysis with details.
4. Possible responses: She will see Cluny elsewhere; she will see the hordes' reaction. She will be angry, upset, furious, etc.

Book Three, Chapter 2, page 65

1. Possible responses: He doesn't like the taste of mice; he's a vegetarian, except for fish; his former best friend is an owl; he is friendly toward shrews.
2. "I"
3. Since hell is supposed to be full of fire, an icicle would exist there only for a moment before it melted; in the same way, Matthias will live only a brief moment in his encounter with Asmodeus.
4. Answers will vary. Some students may cite the importance of forgiveness.

Book Three, Chapter 3, page 66

1. He makes it seem to his followers that it was part of his plan to stop Cheesethief's ambition without even having to raise a finger himself.
2. Answers will vary. Students' speculations should have some grounding in what could and would be realistically done in the woods.
3. She means an unpleasant one and possibly is referring to something that is literally hot.

Book Three, Chapter 4, page 66

1. Answers will vary. Students should support their opinion with reasons.
2. Students should explain the look-out and relay system in detail. Answers about Mingo's death will vary. Students may feel that it was inevitable.
3. Answers will vary. Students may think that alone and unprotected in Asmodeus's territory, she is doomed.

Book Three, Chapter 5, page 67

1. It would be too dangerous for the horde, the Abbey, and the countryside—he would risk destroying what he is fighting to take over.
2. Answers will vary. Many students may think that Cluny is at least temporarily insane. Students should support their surmises with details.
3. Possible response: It would have been too late to stop the horde from entering and taking over Redwall.

Book Three, Chapter 6, page 68

1. Students may mention finding Asmodeus without awakening him; staying calm; coping with Guosim's death; getting around Asmodeus's tongue to reach the sword hanging on the tree root.
2. Possible response: look for the marks on the wall and use them to guide myself out.

Book Three, Chapter 7, page 68

1. Cluny's dream reflects realities that he himself does not consciously know.
2. Answers will vary. Students' surmises about what they'll tell Cluny should be consistent with Fangburn's and Killconey's characters as well as with Cluny's.

Book Three, Chapter 8, page 69

1. Answers will vary. Students should support their answers with reasons.
2. Students may comment on the contents—what's mentioned and what isn't—or the sequence. They may note that he doesn't strike for himself or for Cornflower (whose favor he probably still wears).

Test 5: Book Three, Chapters 1–8, page 70

Vocabulary

A.1. Accomplish 2 tasks at one time; Cluny uses it to (falsely) explain how he plotted Cheesethief's demise.
2. Hurt them as much as they hurt us; Winifred says it to inspire the otters.
B.1. They describe Captain Snow.
2. They describe the results of the accidental fire.
3. They describe the phantom mouse of Cluny's dreams.
4. They refer to the "welcome" that the Redwallers give the rats as they come out from their tunnel.
5. They describe the effect Asmodeus has on Log-a-Log and Matthias.

Essay Topics
1. Students should see that *distinct* contains the sound of the word <u>stink</u>. Students may or may not think it was intentional, and should support their opinions with reasons.
2. Some students may feel that once they make a commitment, they can carry it through because they know they've used the process that they support. Others may point out that the decision-making process takes an enormous amount of time.
3. Answers will vary. Students may talk about fate or destiny and connect Matthias's feeling to the riddle which declares that the sword belongs to him.
4. Possible response: It shows the fulfillment of the dream that Matthias voiced in Chapter 1.
5. Answers will vary. Students should support their opinions with facts.
6. Answers will vary. Students should show that they take into account Matthias's likely emotional, physical, and mental state after he kills Asmodeus.
7. Answers will vary. Students should support their conjectures with details.

Book Three, Chapter 9, page 72
1. Answers will vary. Many students will agree that a weapon's value and role depend on who wields it.
2. In this chapter Matthias is surprised by Julian; the shrews are surprised by Julian's greeting; Captain Snow is surprised by Julian's response to his apology.

Book Three, Chapter 10, page 72
1. Answers will vary. Students should support their speculation with reasons.
2. Answers will vary. Students should support their choices with reasons and give a rationale for choosing between evils.
3. Answers will vary. Students should explain their answers.

Book Three, Chapter 11, page 73
1. The celebration of the shrews and Matthias contrasts with the fear brought on by Warbeak's report of the events at the Abbey.
2. Students should mention Cluny's dreams.
3. Answers will vary. Students may suggest multiple surprise attacks, or forces coming from the air and the ground at the same time.

Book Three, Chapter 12, page 73
1. The horde is silent and cooperative with each other.
2. Cluny believes that he will eliminate the possible source of danger to himself.
3. That the shrews and sparrows and Matthias are coming.

Book Three, Chapter 13, page 73
1. There are "wormdoors" in the walls on the east, south, and north sides of the Abbey, which the Sparras will open to allow the shrews onto the Abbey grounds.
2. Answers will vary. Students should support their answers with reasons.

Book Three, Chapter 14, page 74
1. **Yes:** When he says (page 347), "So have I, my son, so have I," he is referring to having "done his task"; and he tells his friends, "Do not be sad, for mine is a peaceful rest."
2. Answers will vary. Students should tell why they do or do not think that the Abbot's decisions are appropriate for these characters. Some students may question the Abbot telling Cornflower to marry Matthias rather than asking her.
3. Answers will vary. Students may wish especially to know Plumpen's fate.
4. Answers will vary. Students should cite their reasoning and the parts of the text that led them to this conclusion.

5. Students may mention the following: that Matthias has fulfilled his dream of becoming a warrior; that the relationship between Matthias and Cornflower has been solidified; that the community within Redwall Abbey and between the Redwallers and their friends and neighbors has been cemented; that the shrews are no longer nomads; that Julian and Captain Snow have been reconciled.

Book Three, Chapter 15, page 75
1. It is summer again; the Abbey is celebrating a feast in honor of the Abbot; Constance is again pulling the cart to transport guests; Alf and Matthias are catching a fish for the feast.
2. Answers will vary. Students should relate their opinions to the text.
3. Answers will vary. Students should identify the criteria they use in judgment.
4. Possible responses: Prequels: stories about Martin and Methuselah and the Abbot when they were younger; Sequels: stories about Mattimeo, Silent Sam, Alf, Tim, and Tess.

Strategy 11: Theme, page 76
1. Answers will vary. Students may refer to the Abbot's last words or to Matthias's finding a place in the world that both serves the community and fulfills his personal dreams.

Strategy 12: Rereading a Book, page 77
1. Students' second reading should in general be smoother and easier than the first since they have already dealt with the large amount of difficult vocabulary. What is lacking in suspense the second time through may be compensated by their ability to take in more of the detail and appreciate more of the artistry used in constructing the text.

Writer's Forum: Book Review, page 78
1. Students should include the title, author, genre, and summary, but should present them in a personalized way and include their own opinion of the work.

Writer's Forum: Compare and Contrast a Book and a Sound Recording, page 79
1. Students should note important differences between the book and the recording, such as the use of a narrator, oral interpretation, and the role of the reader/listener in terms of contributing imaginatively to the experience of the story.

Test 6: Book Three, Chapters 9–15, page 80
Vocabulary
1. These words describe Captain Snow.
2. These words refer to the feast held by Matthias and the shrews.
3. "Hand in hand"; it means that Julian and Captain Snow are completely restored in their friendship.

Essay Topics
1. Possible responses: He is more mature; he has greater self-knowledge; he is more sure of himself; he is more independent; he understands his role in the community; he has gone from meeting a girl to marrying her and becoming a parent.
2. Jacques most often begins with a character's name and then tells what that character is doing. He also uses the sun and references to time (e.g., candles, the Joseph Bell tolling the time, "it was late afternoon.") to mark the passage of time. Sometimes he begins with a setting.
3. Answers will vary. Students should refer both to details in the text and to their personal response.
4. Answers will vary. Students may find the words uplifting, or find that their personal beliefs and attitudes about death are very different from the Abbot's.
5. Possible response: It's a way to tie up loose ends and quickly summarize the activities, achievements, and situations of a large number of characters in a short space.
6. Answers will vary. Students should identify their criteria.
7. Answers will vary. Students should identify their criteria.
8. Answers will vary. Students' reasons should be based on the text and their reaction to it.

English Series

The Straight Forward English S[...]

is designed to measure, teach, review, and master specified English skills: capitalization and punctuat[...] nouns and pronouns; verbs; adjectives and adverb[...] prepositions, conjunctions and interjections; senter[...] clauses and phrases, and mechanics.

Each workbook is a simple, straightforward approa[...] learning English skills. Skills are keyed to major scl[...] textbook adoptions.

Pages are reproducible.

GP-032	Capitalization and Punctuation
GP-033	Nouns and Pronouns
GP-034	Verbs
GP-035	Adjectives and Adverbs
GP-041	Sentences
GP-043	Prepositions, conjunctions, & Interjections

Advanced Series

Large editions

GP-055	Clauses & Phrases
GP-056	Mechanics
GP-075	Grammar & Diagramming Sentences

Discovering Literature Series

The Discovering Literature Series

is designed to develop an appreciation for literature and to improve reading skills. Each guide in the series features an award winning novel and explores a wide range of critical reading skills and literature elements.

GP-076	A Teaching Guide to My Side of the Mountain
GP-077	A Teaching Guide to Where the Red Fern Grows
GP-078	A Teaching Guide to Mrs. Frisby & the Rats of NIMH
GP-079	A Teaching Guide to Island of the Blue Dolphins
GP-093	A Teaching Guide to the Outsiders
GP-094	A Teaching Guide to Roll of Thunder

Challenging Level

GP-090	The Hobbit: A Teaching Guide
GP-091	Redwall: A Teaching Guide
GP-092	The Odyssey: A Teaching Guide
GP-097	The Giver: A Teaching Guide